Nurture The Soul

By

Loni Mendez

ISBN: 1985233339

ISBN-13: 978-1985233331

DEDICATION

This book is dedicated to my adorable and lovable grandson Cristiano Josiah

ACKNOWLEDGEMENTS

I would like to acknowledge God for making me who I am, my parents the late Glasco Morris, Sr. and the late Laura Evans Morris for giving me life, and my three children, Quiana, Harriel, Jr. and Kennedi, for being a major part of my purpose in life.

"If you would not be forgotten as soon as you are dead, either write something worth reading or do something worth writing."
Benjamin Franklin

A NOTE ABOUT THIS BOOK

This book is designed so that you can, on any given day, turn to the corresponding date and read the devotional for that date.

Most of the pages of this book consist of three components: a quote, a section that contains my insight as related to the topic of the quote, and a selected scripture from the Bible.

There are some pages for which I am the author of the quote. On these pages, since they contain my quotes, There is no additional writing in terms of insight. Therefore, these pages only contain two components: my quote, and a selected scripture.

My wish is that when you are weighed down with the heaviness of the world, you will find inspiration in this book; and when you are in seek of motivation, you will pick up this book and find it.

10% of my earnings from this book will be donated to an organization known as Suicide Awareness Voices of Education (www.save.org), which is dedicated to the prevention of suicide.

January 1

"You never know the true value of a moment until it becomes a memory." ***Unknown***

When we are in the midst of a crisis in our lives, we tend to be focused on the impact it has on us at that moment. It's not until much later that we realize that the crisis actually made it possible for us to move in another direction. I always say that it's God's way of nudging us toward where He wants us to go. We've all heard that saying that when God closes one door, He opens another. The next time you are going through something in your life, make an attempt to stay open. Remind yourself that there must be some lesson in the crisis, or some positive outcome that you will recognize down the road.

"'For I know the plans I have for you,' declares the Lord, 'plans to prosper you and not to harm you, plans to give you hope and a future.'" Jeremiah 29:11

January 2

"Real success means creating a life of meaning through service that fulfills your reason for being here." ***Oprah Winfrey***

Most of us have our own definition of what success means. But I believe that God has a plan for us, and that each of us was created to fulfill on a purpose. I once read somewhere that God gives us the gift of life, and in turn, what we do with that life is our gift to Him. Each and every one of us has a calling to be of service to our fellow human beings, using the gifts and talents that He has blessed us with.

"God is not unjust, he will not forget your work and the love you have shown him as you have helped his people and continue to help them." Hebrews 6:10

January 3

"A simple rule I love to remember in life: things that happen in life happen because they were meant to happen; and things that don't happen don't happen because they weren't meant to happen. Can't get any simpler than that!" ***Loni Mendez***

"And we know that in all things God works for the good of those who love him, who have been called according to his purpose." Romans 8:28

January 4

"Be careful what you set your heart upon - for it will surely be yours." ***James A. Baldwin***

I believe that God has given us the power to create using language. On that note, we should be careful of the circumstances that we speak into our lives. Make a conscious effort to speak good, wholesome and positive outcomes and that is what you will cultivate in your life.

"so is my word that goes out from my mouth: It will not return to me empty, but will accomplish what I desire and achieve the purpose for which I sent it." Isaiah 55:11

January 5

"When you wake up every morning thank God for all those things that you have been praying for, even if they have not yet manifested themselves. They are in route to you...God's timing is always perfect!"

Loni Mendez

"Now faith is confidence in what we hope for and assurance about what we do not see." Hebrews 11:1

January 6

"Great minds discuss ideas, average minds discuss events, small minds discuss people."
Eleanor Roosevelt

There are so many times in life that I've had an idea…a pressing idea, and I took immediate action on it. In most of those cases, something significant got created. And then there are those times when I had an idea, and never acted upon it, only to later find out that someone else somewhere in the world had the same idea, actually took action on it, and made something great happen. When you have those revelations, be sure to write them down, discuss them with someone you can trust, consider how you can follow through on them before too much time passes, and most importantly, take action. Don't talk about what everyone else is doing, be one who actually makes things happen. And lastly, never waste your energy gossiping or talking about others!

"Now that you know these things you will be blessed to do them." John 13:17

January 7

"Often times we play the small games in life, for fear that we might not be able to succeed at the bigger ones. But when we focus on those big games that make a difference for others…the giants…the little things tend to fall into place. For example: if you are working to create an event or organization that would feed 10,000 hungry people, believe that if you were up to something like this, the universe would be sure that you are provided with what you need to maintain a life."

Loni Mendez

"A sluggard's appetite is never filled, but the desires of the diligent are fully satisfied." Proverbs 13:4

January 8

"Your comfort zone is your enemy...there is no comfort in the growth zone." ***Unknown***

I believe in the concept that whatever does not grow dies. As living entities, we simply must grow in order to continue to exist. Growth can almost be looked at as the opposite of comfort. So the next time you have that opportunity in front of you, the one that you are afraid to act on because it is out of your comfort zone, consider that moving forward is an integral part of your continued existence, and the plan for your future.

"Your beginnings will seem humble, so prosperous will your future be." Job 8:7

January 9

"Who we become in life is shaped by every one of the experiences we are having." ***Tyler Perry***

When we are going through something, we tend to visit the question, "why?" During these times we don't usually look for the blessing, nor the lesson in the situation or event. However, in hindsight, we often see all the benefits of that same event….all the things that wouldn't have happened were it not for that situation that seemed so bad at the time that it occurred. I believe in the concept that "what doesn't kill us will make us stronger. All of those mishaps and bad situations, they all happened for a reason, and it is those events that shape us into the champions that God wants us to become. The reality is that things don't necessarily happen **to** us, they happen **for** us.

"But now, O LORD, you are our father; we are the clay, and you our potter; and we all are the work of your hand."
Isaiah 64:8

January 10

"Yesterday is history, tomorrow is a mystery, today is a gift...that's why they call it the present."
Kung Fu Panda

The best place for us to live is in the present. We will never be able to bring the things or the people of our past back. But we can forever store their memories in our hearts. At the other end of this spectrum is the idea of living in the future, which is also counter-productive. While we have to plan for the future, spending time worrying about a future that has not yet transpired results in unnecessary stress. There is an amusing quote that jokingly points out how worrying is an effective method of prevention because 90% of what we worry about happening, actually never happens. When we focus on being present in the moment, right here...right now...we leave anxiety behind and enter the space of peace.

"Cast all your anxiety on Him, because He cares for you."
1 Peter 5:7

January 11

"Happiness does not depend on external conditions, it is governed by our mental attitude." ***Dale Carnegie***

Happiness is not found, it's created. Choose to be happy today. The power to make that choice is a power that no one can take away from you.

"I have told you this so that my joy may be in you and that your joy may be complete." John 15:11

January 12

"If you don't know where you're going any path will get you there." ***Unknown***

Setting goals for the future is critical. This should be an ongoing process in our lives. Often times, people are afraid to set goals for fear that they may not reach them. There have been times when I've set a goal, and worked diligently to accomplish it by a certain time, and failed. But when I look back, I can see the value in the overall experience. Even though I didn't reach the goal on the first attempt, I learned so much throughout the process of working to get there. Goals provide a road map that moves us forward in life. Without them, life can be like a bumper car ride with us randomly bumping into people, experiences, etc. with no intention.

"He fulfills the desires of those who fear him;
he hears their cry and saves them." Psalms 145:19

January 13

"The only person you should try to be better than is the person you were yesterday." ***Unknown***

When we compare ourselves to others we rob ourselves of our own greatness. God created each of us as a unique individual who is whole, perfect and complete. Hands down, there is no comparison to you. Only you can walk your walk and live your purpose. Living a balanced life includes both being proud of who you are and what you stand for, and encouraging others to walk their walk and live their purpose.

"Each one should test their own actions. Then they can take pride in themselves alone, without comparing themselves to someone else," Galatians 6:4

January 14

"The power and reach of your motivation dictate the power and reach of your success." ***Gary Keller***

Whenever you set a goal, a good way to stay motivated is to remain focused by keeping your eye on the end result. One of the things that I do is visualize myself living the scenarios that will take place when I reach that goal. The bible refers to that end result as the "fruit of our labor." If you practice visualization, nothing can stop you from achieving whatever it is that you want. And let me just add that the very fact that you have this desire in your heart and mind is an indication that you are on the right path.

"You will eat the fruit of your labor; blessings and prosperity will be yours." Psalms 128:2

January 15

"The greatest challenge in life is discovering who you are. The second greatest is being happy with what you find." ***Unknown***

Although many may not be aware of it, each of us have a purpose on this earth. God has blessed us with gifts and talents that we will use to make a difference for others. Even if you are not yet sure what your gifts are, or what your purpose is, be proud of who you are, and trust the path that God has set for you.

"For this reason I remind you to fan into flame the gift of God, which is in you through the laying on of my hands."
2 Timothy 1:6

January 16

"In the end, it's not the years in your life that count. It's the life in your years."
Abraham Lincoln

Life is a gift, and it's up to us to make the most of it. One of the things I always tell people about myself is that when my life is over, I will have lived it to the absolute fullest. Make each day on this journey a fulfilling and productive one, and commit to making a difference for each and every person you encounter.

"For the Spirit God gave us does not make us timid, but gives us power, love and self-discipline."
2 Timothy 1:7

January 17

"Decide. Commit. Act. Succeed. Repeat."
Tim Grover

God has given each of us the power to speak things into existence. We can literally design our lives, and it all starts with deciding what we want. Once we identify what we want for ourselves, what there is to do is set goals, and then take action.

"I can do all things through Christ who strengthens me."
Philippians 4:13

January 18

"Never let failures, disappointments or circumstances stop you from living your life with passion. Each day is a new day with new opportunities for great things to happen!"
Loni Mendez

"The Lord has done it this very day; let us rejoice today and be glad." Psalms 118:24

January 19

"If you cannot absorb failure, you will never meet success." ***Unknown***

Our failures teach us valuable lessons that are an integral part of our journey. The key to success is to embrace failure and to recognize that when we encounter failures, we have simply identified what doesn't work.

"for though the righteous fall seven times, they rise again, but the wicked stumble when calamity strikes."
Proverbs 24:16

January 20

"Gratitude makes sense of our past, brings peace for today and creates a vision for tomorrow."
Melody Beattie

I once heard a famous public figure credit gratitude for cultivating abundance in our lives. When I am working with my coachees, I always encourage them to remove the focus from the things that make them sad or make them feel inadequate. I encourage them to instead focus on all the things that they have to be grateful for. When we are grateful, we send the message to the universe that we want more of those things that we express gratitude for.

"Give thanks to the Lord, for he is good; his love endures forever." 1 Chronicles 16:34

January 21

"When you have God in your life, you can stand fearless in the face of any and every challenge!"
Loni Mendez

"Finally, be strong in the Lord and in his mighty power."
Ephesians 6:10

January 22

"To my fellow leaders: when you find yourself in a situation where the people around you do not have clarity and are instead operating from a place of confusion, it's time for you to step into your leadership, be the space of clarity and the voice of reason, and set a powerful intention....and without judgement!"

Loni Mendez

"Remember your leaders, who spoke the word of God to you. Consider the outcome of their way of life and imitate their faith." Hebrews 13:7

January 23

"Too many people buy things they don't need, with money they don't have, to impress people they don't even know" ***from the book "Rich Dad Poor Dad"***

The fastest way to diminish your blessings and accomplishments is to compare yourself to others. Each of us will realize success according to God's timeline. Don't worry about other people's success or material possessions. Instead, focus on your own life, journey, blessings and accomplishments.

"Am I now trying to win the approval of human beings, or of God? Or am I trying to please people? If I were still trying to please people, I would not be a servant of Christ."
Galatians 1:10

January 24

"The greatest tragedy in life is not death, but a life without a purpose." ***Dr. Myles Munroe***

God has given each of us gifts and talents that are to be used to contribute to our fellow human beings. When we are able to identify these gifts and talents, it results in lives that are lived "on purpose."

"great are your purposes and mighty are your deeds. Your eyes are open to the ways of all mankind; you reward each person according to their conduct and as their deeds deserve." Jeremiah 32:19

January 25

"When you can chart your own course in life in spite of what society has dictated as the norm, not only is it a gift, but it distinguishes you from other people. One of the caveats is that there will be many who do not have the space or the capacity to walk with you."

Loni Mendez

"And who knows but that you have come to your royal position for such a time as this?" Esther 4:14

January 26

"When you start your day from a place of possibility, you automatically leave space for miracles to happen." ***Loni Mendez***

"But now, Lord, what do I look for? My hope is in you." Psalms 39:7

January 27

"Ladies, not every man who wants to be with you can accept the path that God has set for you to walk. When you are secure with who you are, and you know your purpose in life, not only will you not be distracted by the counterfeits, you will recognize when the one who is for you enters your life. There will be no question and no doubts...he will be unmistakable." ***Loni Mendez***

"Commit to the Lord whatever you do,
and he will establish your plans." Proverbs 16:3

January 28

"Make today count by doing your best. Even if your best today doesn't measure up to your best yesterday, today's version of your best is good enough." ***Unknown***

Each night, when I lay my head down to go to sleep, what I am most proud of is reflecting on my day, and realizing that I actually made a difference for someone. Sometimes it's one person, and sometimes it's more than one. Sometimes, its many people. That is my confirmation that I did my absolute best that day.

"Do your best to present yourself to God as one approved, a worker who does not need to be ashamed and who correctly handles the word of truth." 2 Timothy 2:15

January 29

"Your greatest responsibility is to love yourself and to know that you are loved." ***Unknown***

If you ever question whether or not you are loved, just remember God's grace and mercy, and thank Him for all of the blessings that he showers upon you every single day.

"I praise you because I am fearfully and wonderfully made; your works are wonderful, I know that full well."
Psalms 139:14

January 30

"You were born an original don't die a copy."
John Mason

God made us each unique, with different gifts and talents. Identify those gifts and use them to help other people, and you will find that doing so is both fulfilling and rewarding.

"Each of you should use whatever gift you have received to serve others, as faithful stewards of God's grace in its various forms." 1 Peter 4:10

January 31

"The greatest contribution we can make to the wellbeing of those in our lives is to have peace in our own hearts." ***David Simon***

When I left the corporate world to start my own business, I was walking away from six figures and into the unknown. However, I realized after years of working in a toxic environment that when it comes to your peace of mind, sometimes money is the factor that should be given the least amount of consideration.

'Peace I leave with you; my peace I give you. I do not give to you as the world gives. Do not let your hearts be troubled and do not be afraid." John 14:27

February 1

"Two things define you: your patience when you have nothing, and your attitude when you have everything." ***Unknown***

It is so easy to be great when all of your needs are met, and you are living in abundance. But when times get tough, and you are facing uncertainty about what's ahead, that is when you must have faith and patience. The God who is with you in times of abundance and success, is the same God that is with you during those troubled times. He will never let you down, and He will surely walk you through those troubles, to a place of victory, on His timetable.

"Humble yourselves before the Lord, and He will lift you up." James 4:10

February 2

"We are given a voice to utilize it, share it, connect with others, and tell our stories."
Kim Sisto Robinson

Those of us who are out here in the world contributing to others by sharing our stories are summoned to do so. Not everyone has the wherewithal to use his or her voice. There have been times when I've found out months, or even years later that I made a difference for someone through my words. Whether you find out about it or not does not matter, but that you had an impact on that person does. If you are someone who has a testimony, share your story, as it could make a difference for that person who really needs to hear it. You never know what your words can or will provide for someone who is in earshot.

"From the fruit of their lips people are filled with good things, and the work of their hands brings them reward."
Proverbs 12:14

February 3

"Even though our lives are not our own, and our time here on earth is temporary, life is a gift....live your life on purpose and enjoy your stay!"
Loni Mendez

"I know that there is nothing better for people than to be happy and to do good while they live." Ecclesiastes 3:12

February 4

"If you don't let your past die, your past won't let you live." ***Unknown***

I believe that when we hold on to the events of the past, if prevents us from being able to move forward. Furthermore, moving on does not mean that you will forget those events, it simply means that you acknowledge that holding on to them stops you from making progress, and that you allow yourself to be free of the restraint that they have had on you.

"Forget the former things; do not dwell on the past."
Isaiah 43:18

February 5

"On good teams coaches hold players accountable, on great teams players hold coaches accountable." ***Joe Demars***

When we are held accountable, we accept responsibility for our actions. This is a very powerful concept and practice that is necessary for competent leadership. Without a true understanding of what it means to be held accountable, there can be no demonstration of leadership.

"So then, each of us will give an account of ourselves to God." Romans 14:12

February 6

"If you set your goals ridiculously high and it's a failure, you will fail above everyone else's success." ***James Cameron***

Setting goals is an integral part of life, they support our growth and development, and help us to become the people God meant for us to be. However, we must keep in mind that if we set a goal and we do not succeed in reaching it, we can always change our strategy and try something different. Failure is simply identifying one more way of doing something that doesn't work.

"The plans of the diligent lead to profit as surely as haste leads to poverty." Proverbs 21:5

February 7

"We cannot learn without pain." ***Aristotle***

No one wants to experience pain, but it is an inevitable part of life. When dealing with painful events in life, it's not an easy task, but we must try to focus on the lessons learned from the experience. This will not eliminate the pain, but it will help to strengthen you. Ultimately, context is decisive.

"The Lord is close to the brokenhearted and saves those who are crushed in spirit." Psalms 34:18

February 8

"A journey of 1000 miles begins with a single step." ***Lao Tzu***

When I work with people in my professional organizing business, one of the first thing I teach them is not to look at the entire organizing project as they begin. This would make the task seem even more daunting than it is. But if we just focus on the part of the task that is currently at hand, it will appear much more doable. Then, what there is to do is to continue to focus on each part of the task, one part at a time, until you have completed the entire task.

"Therefore do not worry about tomorrow, for tomorrow will worry about itself. Each day has enough trouble of its own." Matthew 6:34

February 9

"Happiness is when what you think, what you say, and what you do are in harmony."
Mahatma Gandhi

Happiness is not found, nor can anyone give or gift it to you. Instead, it is created from within. Once we realize that no relationship, job or material possession can make us happy, we will begin the journey of discovering how to cultivate our happiness from the inside out.

"With joy you will draw water from the wells of salvation." Isaiah 12:3

February 10

"When you spread love, you diminish hate."
Loni Mendez

"Whoever does not love does not know God, because God is love." 1 John 4:8

February 11

"Your job is not to seek the things that you want in life, but to discover how you are subconsciously blocking them." ***Unknown***

So often, we are not aware that our thoughts are preventing us from reaching our goals. When you are working to accomplish something, remember to focus on that favorable outcome, and not on the possibility of failure. The law of attraction is very powerful, and does not recognize when you do not want a particular outcome. It only recognizes your constant focus on that outcome. Therefore, we must focus our thoughts on the outcome that we desire.

"Finally, brothers and sisters, whatever is true, whatever is noble, whatever is right, whatever is pure, whatever is lovely, whatever is admirable—if anything is excellent or praiseworthy—think about such things."
Philippians 4:8

February 12

"No matter how dark it gets, the sun will shine again." ***Unknown***

After losing my baby sister, who was only 46 years old to domestic violence, the statement above is what I used to recite to myself over and over. While we will never forget our loved ones, and even though the pain never goes away completely, it will eventually subside if we remain present to the beautiful memories of our loved ones.

"I have told you these things, so that in me you may have peace. In this world you will have trouble. But take heart! I have overcome the world." John 16:33

February 13

"Once you get good at managing your expectations of other people, nothing really shocks or surprises you anymore."
Loni Mendez

"bless those who curse you, pray for those who mistreat you." Luke 6:28

February 14

"To have courage is not to be without fear, it is to act in spite of the fear." ***Unknown***

FEAR is False Evidence Appearing Real. Don't allow the fear of something that hasn't happened, and probably never will happen, to stop you from moving forward

"Be strong and courageous. Do not be afraid or terrified because of them, for the Lord your God goes with you; he will never leave you nor forsake you." Deuteronomy 31:6

February 15

"The best way to find yourself is to lose yourself in the service of others." ***Mahatma Gandhi***

Doing for other people has always helped to take my mind off of my problems. Being of service takes the focus off of you and points it toward those in need.

"You, my brothers and sisters, were called to be free. But do not use your freedom to indulge the flesh; rather, serve one another humbly in love." Galatians 5:13

February 16

"The future belongs to those who believe in the beauty of their dreams." ***Eleanor Roosevelt***

Never be afraid to dream. That is the beginning of the accomplishment of your goals. Dream, set a goal, take action, trust in God, know that He will order your steps, and you cannot fail.

"May he give you the desire of your heart and make all your plans succeed." *Psalms 20:4*

February 17

"Many of life's failures are people who did not realize how close they were to success when they gave up." ***Thomas A. Edison***

When you are working on accomplishing something major, force yourself to stay the course, even when things get tough. If you quit, you will never know if that next step you would have taken would have been the critical step that would bring that major accomplishment into fruition.

"Let us not become weary in doing good, for at the proper time we will reap a harvest if we do not give up."
Galatians 6:9

February 18

"The only impossible journey is the one you'll never begin." ***Tony Robbins***

I always tell my coaching clients that when they are facing a monumental task, just get started, and let the momentum build from there. We often put the things that we want off because they seem overwhelming. But if we can just take that first step, the wheel will start turning, and we will find ourselves moving closer to that goal, little by little.

"Rise up; this matter is in your hands. We will support you, so take courage and do it." Ezra 10:4

February 19

"Life isn't about finding yourself, life is about creating yourself." ***George Bernard Shaw***

Throughout my life, I have started over from nothing, or almost nothing more than once. Some may see starting from nothing after you've already been established as an encounter with failure. But for me, it's an opportunity to re-invent yourself. In the end, I was actually better off, accomplishing things that would never have been possible without the losses I took that prepared me. Put your trust in Him, as sometimes, loss is a prerequisite to greatness.

"God is our refuge and strength, an ever-present help in trouble." Psalms 46:1

February 20

"Clothes won't change the world, the women who wear them will." ***Anne Klein***

Many people have a hard time detaching themselves from material things. Deep inside, they feel as if "things" make them who they are…the clothes they wear, the car they drive, the house they live in. But in reality, those things are superficial and cannot dictate nor can they change who we really are. What makes a person is the condition of their heart and the authenticity of their soul.

"Set your minds on things above, not on earthly things."
Colossians 3:2

February 21

"You become what you believe."
Oprah Winfrey

When we have the power and the courage to believe in ourselves, coupled with the belief in God, there is no limit to what we can accomplish.

"In their hearts humans plan their course, but the Lord establishes their steps." Proverbs 16:9

February 22

"Too many of us are not living our dreams
because we are living our fears."
Les Brown

When we are afraid to go after what we want in life, we allow fear to shape our lives and our futures. Don't be afraid to try, for if you fail, you can always try something different. The next time around you might get to where you are trying to go.

*"I sought the Lord, and he answered me;
he delivered me from all my fears." Psalms 34:4*

February 23

"In a world where you can be anything, be kind."
Unknown

In today's world, aggression seems to be on autopilot for so many people. Rather than being that person who cuts someone off or refuses to let someone in on the road, be the person who is gracious enough to slow down and be kind to your fellow human beings. Hold the door for someone, smile at that person you pass in the hallway. It doesn't cost anything, and you would be surprised at the difference it makes for that other person.

"Therefore, as God's chosen people, holy and dearly loved, clothe yourselves with compassion, kindness, humility, gentleness and patience." Colossians 3:12

February 24

"There are no shortcuts to any place worth going." ***Beverly Sills***

Instant gratification seems to be a popular theme of this era. But what we all need to realize is that more often than not, success comes only after we pay our dues in time, effort and hard work.

"The end of a matter is better than its beginning, and patience is better than pride." Ecclesiastes 7:8

February 25

"Those who are happiest are those who do the most for others." ***Booker T. Washington***

I am often asked why I have so many business ventures, and how I am able to manage it all. When you make your life about making a difference for others, there is no limit to what you can accomplish.

"Each of you should use whatever gift you have received to serve others, as faithful stewards of God's grace in its various forms." 1 Peter 4:10

February 26

"Once you choose hope anything's possible."
Christopher Reeve

When we are working to accomplish something, not only must we have faith that it will manifest, but we must also grasp and hold on to hope.

"I pray that the eyes of your heart may be enlightened in order that you may know the hope to which he has called you, the riches of his glorious inheritance in his holy people," Ephesians 1:18

February 27

"If a man wants an independent woman, he must be willing to share his power with her."
Loni Mendez

"She speaks with wisdom, and faithful instruction is on her tongue." Proverbs 31:26

February 28

"When the wrong people leave your life, the right things start to happen." ***Zig Ziglar***

I can honestly recall times in my life when I was dating the wrong man, and it seemed as if nothing in my life was working. As soon as those relationships ended, I began to prosper.

"Walk with the wise and become wise, for a companion of fools suffers harm." Proverbs 13:20

March 1

"Happiness is an inside job, don't assign anyone else that much power over your life." ***Unknown***

I realized many moons ago that nothing outside of me can make us happy…no human being, no material possession, no job or anything else. It is up to us to create our own happiness from withing.

"A cheerful heart is good medicine, but a crushed spirit dries up the bones." Proverbs 17:22

March 2

"Love always wins over hate."
Unknown

There is so much hatred in the world today that it seems as if people have forgotten that not only are we all human beings, but we are all one.

"The second is this: 'Love your neighbor as yourself. There is no commandment greater than these.'" Mark 12:31

March 3

"You can't build a reputation on what you're going to do." ***Henry Ford***

I have a good friend who said to me once that procrastination is the biggest nation. I can honestly agree with this when I think of the many people I've come across as I go about my daily activities who use all their energy talking about what they are going to do, but actually never get around to doing it. My remedy for this is to minimize the chatter, bring the things you want to do into existence by writing them down and find an accountability buddy to help keep you on track.

"If anyone, then, knows the good they ought to do and doesn't do it, it is sin for them." James 4:17

March 4

"True friends are like diamonds – bright, beautiful, valuable and always in style."
Nicole Richie

While I have tons of associates, I keep my circle small. I can count the number of people in my life whom I consider friends with one hand. A true friend is someone you can call when you have an emergency at 3:00 AM and know they will be there to support you.

"The righteous choose their friends carefully, but the way of the wicked leads them astray." Proverbs 12:26

March 5

"Only in the darkness can you see the stars."
Dr. Martin Luther King, Jr.

Nobody likes going through tough times, but the fact is, if we never face adversity, we would certainly not appreciate those times when all is going well.

"Is anyone among you in trouble? Let them pray. Is anyone happy? Let them sing songs of praise."
Jeremiah 5:13

March 6

"Every defeat, every heartbreak, every loss, contains its own seed, its own lesson on how to improve your performance next time."
Malcolm X

It is of great benefit to focus on the lessons learned from our setback and misfortunes. By doing this, we empower ourselves instead of giving power to the situation or circumstance.

"Let the wise listen and add to their learning, and let the discerning get guidance-" Proverbs 1:5

March 7

"You get in life what you have the courage to ask for." ***Oprah Winfrey***

One of the things that I learned in life is that anything is possible, but we will never know if we will be granted what we want if we do not ask. One of my favorite lines is, "It's just a request, what's the worst thing that can happen."

"Therefore I tell you, whatever you ask for in prayer, believe that you have received it, and it will be yours."
Mark 11:24

March 8

"A goal properly set is halfway reached."
Zig Ziglar

I recall one year I participated in a year-end event, and the participants had to answer a series of questions about our accomplishments for the year. In that event, I realized that I hadn't accomplished much that year, because I hadn't set any goals. This speaks to how important it is to set goals!

*"Commit to the Lord whatever you do,
and he will establish your plans." Proverbs 16:3*

March 9

"Life is like riding a bicycle, to keep your balance you must keep moving."
Albert Einstein

In the face of a major setback, the best thing you can do is briefly reflect on what didn't work so that you can come up with another plan, and keep moving forward.

"Let your eyes look straight ahead; fix your gaze directly before you." Proverbs 4:25

March 10

"Never get so busy making a living that you forget to make a life." ***Dolly Parton***

In order to generate an extraordinary life, we must take the best possible care of ourselves. One way to do that is to make sure that we make time for the people we enjoy being with and the things that we enjoy doing.

"The Lord has done it this very day;
let us rejoice today and be glad." Psalms 118:24

March 11

"When you have faith in yourself, you don't need others to believe in you." ***Unknown***

Faith will take you further than approval or validation from another person ever will.

"for the Lord will be at your side and will keep your foot from being snared." Proverbs 3:26

March 12

"The ones who think they are crazy enough to change the world are the ones who do."
Steve Jobs

Each one of us plays a role in making the world a better place. Our job is to listen to that inner spirit which is where we will discover what that actually looks like for each of us as the unique individuals that we are.

"For we are God's handiwork, created in Christ Jesus to do good works, which God prepared in advance for us to do." Ephesians 2:10

March 13

"Change is never easy, but it's always possible."
Barack Obama

Living from what's possible opens countless doors for those who may have given up hope.

"I know that you can do all things;
no purpose of yours can be thwarted." Job 42:2

March 14

"Don't settle for a relationship that won't let you be yourself." ***Oprah Winfrey***

When you are sure about who you are, and God has revealed to you what you purpose is in life, you will be comfortable with always being true to yourself. This is a gift that no one can take away from you.

"Do not conform to the pattern of this world, but be transformed by the renewing of your mind. Then you will be able to test and approve what God's will is—his good, pleasing and perfect will." Romans 12:2

March 15

"You are a gift! God made each of us whole, perfect and complete just the way we are. So if a person can't allow you the freedom to be who you are, why grace them with your presence? They don't deserve to be in your space." ***Loni Mendez***

"Every good and perfect gift is from above, coming down from the Father of the heavenly lights, who does not change like shifting shadows." James 1:17

March 16

"Take care of your body, it's the only place you have to live." ***Jim Rohn***

Many times, we get so caught up in trying to do for everyone else, that we neglect ourselves. If we make sure to take care of ourselves first, then we will have the wherewithal to support and care for others.

"After all, no one ever hated their own body, but they feed and care for their body, just as Christ does the church—"
Ephesians 5:29

March 17

"We cannot solve our problems with the same thinking we used when we created them."
Albert Einstein

The old saying that if you do what you've always done, you'll get what you always got is the absolute truth. When we are unhappy with the results in our lives, we must take a look at how we got where we are, and then make the commitment to do something different in order to produce a different result.

"See, I am doing a new thing! Now it springs up; do you not perceive it? I am making a way in the wilderness and streams in the wasteland." Isaiah 43:19

March 18

"If you are going through hell, keep going."
Winston Churchill

In dealing with the day-to-day challenges of life, no matter how dire things might look, keep going. If you quit you will never know just how close you were to getting through that difficult time.

"But as for you, be strong and do not give up, for your work will be rewarded." 2 Chronicles 15:7

March 19

"No man is an island but a true leader is willing and able to walk alone when warranted."
Loni Mendez

"Give careful thought to the paths for your feet and be steadfast in all your ways." Proverbs 4:26

March 20

"Success isn't about how much money you make, it's about the difference you make in people's lives." ***Michelle Obama***

While living requires a paycheck, we have the ability to use the gifts that God gave us to make a difference for others simultaneously.

"for God's gifts and his call are irrevocable."
Romans 11:29

March 21

"Every choice in life either moves you forward or keeps you stuck." ***Oprah Winfrey***

When I look back over my life, I can honestly say that there have been single decisions that I've made that ended up changing the trajectory of my life, and I had no idea that they would at the time that I made them. When your inner spirit is telling you to make a particular move, take action. In hindsight you will be glad that you did.

"Listen to advice and accept discipline, and at the end you will be counted among the wise." Proverbs 19:20

March 22

"A person who never made a mistake never tried anything new." ***Albert Einstein***

Don't be so afraid to fail that you give up trying. When you make an attempt and you do not succeed, you have not failed, you have simply identified one more approach that does not work.

"though he may stumble, he will not fall, for the Lord upholds him with his hand." Psalms 37:24

March 23

"Discipline is choosing between what you want now and what you want most."
Abraham Lincoln

When you are truly committed to what you want to create for your future, it provides the motivation to do what needs to be done today in order to produce those results.

"Like a city whose walls are broken through is a person who lacks self-control." Proverbs 25:28

March 24

"Setting goals is the first step in turning the invisible into the visible." ***Tony Robbins***

Writing down your goals puts them into existence, giving them a life and granting them the space to become realities.

"The plans of the diligent lead to profit as surely as haste leads to poverty." Proverbs 21:5

March 25

"May your choices reflect your hopes not your fears." ***Nelson Mandela***

The result of living from a place of possibility on a daily basis is drastically different than what your life looks like when your day-to-day decisions are driven by fear.

"Fear not, for I am with you; be not dismayed, for I am your God; I will strengthen you, I will help you, I will uphold you with my righteous right hand." Isaiah 41:10

March 26

"Our humanity is the one thing that we all have in common." ***Melinda Gates***

We are human, all God's creations, and all of the same spirit. If you take a good look, you will see yourself in fellow human beings, and therefore, be more relatable to them.

"All the believers were together and had everything in common." Acts 2:44

March 27

"If you start today, you'll start to see results one day earlier than you would if you start tomorrow."
Unknown

Developing a sense of urgency is a skill that serves us well when it comes to making the most of that time that God grants us each day and getting the things done that matter most to us.

"Teach us to number our days, that we may gain a heart of wisdom." Psalms 90:12

March 28

"We may encounter many defeats but we must not be defeated." ***Maya Angelou***

Challenges are meant to be overcome, for they teach us valuable lessons that we must learn on the path to success.

"Be on your guard; stand firm in the faith; be courageous; be strong" 1 Corinthians 16:13

March 29

"You will never have to force anything that is truly meant to be." ***Loni Mendez***

"your kingdom come, your will be done, on earth as it is in heaven." Matthew 6:10

March 30

"The two most important days of your life are the day you were born, and the day you find out why."
Mark Twain

Our purpose in life is predetermined. Some people discover what their purpose is at an early age. However, for some of us, it is not until well into adulthood that our purpose is revealed to us.

"But I have raised you up for this very purpose, that I might show you my power and that my name might be proclaimed in all the earth." Exodus 9:16

March 31

"If you are in the position to lend a hand to a fellow human being, regardless of whether it is through a gesture, the donation of a resource, or a financial contribution, don't worry about how big or how small it is, or how much or little you have to give, just know that taking that action is already beyond measurement." ***Loni Mendez***

"Do not neglect to do good and to share what you have, for such sacrifices are pleasing to God." Hebrews 13:16

April 1

"Be happy with what you have, while you pursue what you want." ***Unknown***

The best way to attract more of what you want in your life is to be grateful for what you already have.

"give thanks in all circumstances; for this is God's will for you in Christ Jesus." 1 Thessalonians 5:18

April 2

"I've failed over and over and over again in my life, and that is why I succeed."
Michael Jordan

The proven strategy for overcoming failure is to keep trying until you get it right.

"Stand firm, and you will win life." Luke 21:19

April 3

"Being true to yourself is the essence of personal success." ***Unknown***

Success looks different for each one of us. There is no gratification in working hard to achieve goals that someone else felt were right for you. Genuine success is the achievement of the goals you set for yourself.

Whatever you do, work at it with all your heart, as working for the Lord, not for human masters,"
Colossians 3:23

April 4

"Wealth is not about having a lot of money, it's about having a lot of options." ***Chris Rock***

When you begin to generate all or part of your own income, you are heading in the right direction. No matter how high your salary may be, it is unlikely that you will attain wealth working for someone else.

"By wisdom a house is built, and through understanding it is established;" Proverbs 24:3

April 5

"Repetition is the mother of skill."
Tony Robbins

When misfortune happens in life, and we move through without learning the lesson that was meant for us, it's no wonder that situations continue to occur until we are able to experience the growth necessary for us to move on.

"Whatever you have learned or received or heard from me, or seen in me—put it into practice. And the God of peace will be with you." Philippians 4:9

April 6

"When you are destined for greatness, you must walk the path that God has set for you, making a difference for those who are in need of what you have to contribute." ***Loni Mendez***

"In the same way, let your light shine before others, that they may see your good deeds and glorify your Father in heaven." Matthew 5:16

April 7

"The best way to predict the future is to create it."
Peter Drucker

When you are bold enough to take the action that supports what you want in your future, you get to enjoy the victory of living your life by design rather than by default.

"This is the confidence we have in approaching God: that if we ask anything according to his will, he hears us."
1 John 5:14

April 8

"Integrity is doing the right thing even when no one is watching." ***C.S. Lewis***

When you do things that you know are wrong, there will always be a consequence. So, treat people the way that you want to be treated, and make every effort to keep your word.

"Whoever walks in integrity walks securely, but whoever takes crooked paths will be found out."
Proverbs 10:9

April 9

"The best way to give away your power is thinking you don't have any." ***Unknown***

God gave each and every one of us the power to create through our language, which starts with our thoughts. When we doubt this by succumbing to either our uncertainty or other people's ambiguity, we are basically giving that power away.

"Let your conversation be always full of grace, seasoned with salt, so that you may know how to answer everyone." Colossians 4:6

April 10

"Either you run the day or the day runs you."
Jim Rohn

When you arise each day, make a conscious decision regarding which items on your agenda take precedence. While you may not be able to accomplish all that you want, you can prioritize, making your day as productive as possible.

"Our people must learn to devote themselves to doing what is good, in order to provide for urgent needs and not live unproductive lives." Titus 3:14

April 11

"Help others achieve their dreams and you will achieve yours." ***Les Brown***

If you want more love in your life, show more love to the people around you. If you want people to believe in you, believe in them. In just about every context I can think of, we really do reap what we sow.

"not looking to your own interests but each of you to the interests of the others." Philippians 2:4

April 12

"Once we realize that our existence is intimately connected to making a difference for others, we develop the ability to focus on having an impact on our fellow human beings every single day."

Loni Mendez

"Do not withhold good from those to whom it is due, when it is in your power to act." Proverbs 3:27

April 13

"Intelligence plus character, that is the goal of true education." ***Dr. Martin Luther King***

Learning through an institution is by no means the only way to educate yourself. Life has many learning experiences to offer, including but not limited to reading, traveling, exposure to other cultures, and through conversations with other people.

"Hold on to instruction, do not let it go; guard it well, for it is your life." Proverbs 4:13

April 14

"When the world says 'give up,' hope says 'try it one more time.'" ***Dr. Michelle Bengtson***

When you are taking on those giants that are unavoidable in life, there will always be a wide range of options for getting to the other side, but giving up should never be one of them.

"Be strong and take heart, all you who hope in the Lord."
Psalms 31:24

April 15

"You are the CEO of your life. hire, fire and promote accordingly." ***Unknown***

The energy that you allow in your space is a major ingredient in the recipe for success. Be careful about who you share your aspirations with, choosing people who will support you and lift you up. Beware of the naysayers and those who will be quick to share their reasons why you can't or won't accomplish your goals. These decisions have a direct impact on your results.

"In the name of the Lord Jesus Christ, we command you, brothers and sisters, to keep away from every believer who is idle and disruptive and does not live according to the teaching you received from us." 2 Thessalonians 3:6

April 16

"It may not be necessary or even possible to forget some of the things that were done to you. But when you give grace to those who have done them by practicing forgiveness, you begin the healing process for yourself." ***Loni Mendez***

"Be kind and compassionate to one another, forgiving each other, just as in Christ God forgave you."
Ephesians 4:32

April 17

"There are no secrets to success. It is the result of preparation, hard work and learning from failure."
Colin Powell

As human beings, we would all love to take the shortcut when it comes to achieving our goals and living our dreams, but a shortcut doesn't actually exist. However, rather than there being only one route, there are countless paths to success. The caveat is that each and every one of them consists of certain critical elements that cannot be avoided.

"The hardworking farmer should be the first to receive a share of the crops." 2 Timothy 2:6

April 18

"Life is like riding a bicycle, to keep your balance you need to keep moving."
Albert Einstein

With God's guidance, we are able to move forward and make progress in spite of our doubts or fears.

"I will instruct you and teach you in the way you should go; I will counsel you with my loving eye on you."
Psalms 32:8

April 19

"The art of being happy lies in the power of extracting happiness from common things."
Henry Ward Beecher

Sometimes the smallest and simplest things make me happy. But love that this is who I am.

"sorrowful, yet always rejoicing; poor, yet making many rich; having nothing, and yet possessing everything."
2 Corinthians 6:10

April 20

"Small acts, when multiplied by millions of people, can transform the world."
Howard Zinn

Imagine what the world would be like if each of us made being kind to one another a priority.

"Therefore, as we have opportunity, let us do good to all people, especially to those who belong to the family of believers." Galatians 6:10

April 21

"The strong individual is the one who asks for help when he needs it." ***Rona Barrett***

For many years, I used to be adamant about not asking anyone for help, but as I became older and wiser, I realized that not only is it OK to ask for help, but looking after each other and helping one another is what God has instructed us to do.

"Carry each other's burdens, and in this way you will fulfill the law of Christ." Galatians 6:2

April 22

"Tough times never last, but tough people do."
Robert H. Shuller

One of my favorite affirmations is *this too shall pass.* No matter how bad things look when I am going through a rough patch, I know that in the end, it will all work out according to God's Divine Plan.

"The righteous cry out, and the Lord hears them; he delivers them from all their troubles." Psalms 34:17

April 23

"Men are taught to apologize for their weaknesses, women are taught to apologize for their strengths." ***Lois Wright***

To all you powerful, independent women, do not allow anyone to make you feel bad about who you are or what you are capable of. If a person cannot accept the real you, then perhaps they are not interested in an authentic friendship or relationship.

"She is clothed with strength and dignity; she can laugh at the days to come." Proverbs 31:25

April 24

"To achieve success, we must plow through one failure after another. Never be embarrassed to share your failures with others. It may inspire them to keep trying." ***Loni Mendez***

"Whoever conceals their sins does not prosper, but the one who confesses and renounces them finds mercy."
Proverbs 28:13

April 25

"God placed the best things in life on the other side of your fear." ***Will Smith***

Never allow your fears to stop you from living the purpose that is at the source of your greatness.

"Do not be anxious about anything, but in every situation, by prayer and petition, with thanksgiving, present your requests to God." Philippians 4:6

April 26

"Unhappiness is not knowing what you want and killing yourself to get it." ***Unknown***

It is impossible to be happy if you are moving through life with no idea of what you want to accomplish on this journey.

*"The heart of the wise inclines to the right,
but the heart of the fool to the left."* Ecclesiastes 10:2

April 27

"There is nothing complicated about equality."
Alice Paul

Being part of a diverse universe is a wonderful thing. But different in no way warrants inequality.

"For God does not show favoritism." Romans 2:11

April 28

"The only source of knowledge is experience."
Albert Einstein

The proven strategy for becoming an expert at something is to eat, sleep and breath it until you are familiar with it inside and out.

"Is not wisdom found among the aged? Does not long life bring understanding?" Job 12:12

April 29

"The purpose of our lives is to be happy."
Dalai Lama

While it is impossible to avoid pain and misfortune, the ultimate goal is to live a joyous, fulfilling and happy life.

"Go, eat your food with gladness, and drink your wine with a joyful heart, for God has already approved what you do." Ecclesiastes 9:7

April 30

"The obscure we always see sooner or later; the obvious always seems to take a little longer."
Edward R. Murrow

Sometimes we lack the ability to see things that are right in front of us, in plain sight. Those are the times when we should be grateful for the perspectives of those who are close to our hearts.

"Open my eyes that I may see wonderful things in your law." Psalms 119:18

May 1

"Failure is not the opposite of success; it's part of success." ***Arianna Huffington***

Failure is such a popular topic because it is the thief of so many people's success. The first step in overcoming this thief is to recognize when it is dictating your actions.

"Have I not commanded you? Be strong and courageous. Do not be afraid; do not be discouraged, for the Lord your God will be with you wherever you go." Joshua 1:9

May 2

"Great things come from hard work and perseverance. No excuses." ***Kobe Bryant***

No matter what is in your past or what obstacles you face today, as human beings we have the power to overcome any challenge. God has granted us that power. With Him in our lives, there is no acceptable excuse for not becoming the best that we possibly can.

"All hard work brings a profit, but mere talk leads only to poverty." Proverbs 14:23

May 3

"Money won't create success, the freedom to make it will." ***Nelson Mandela***

I am a huge fan of the concept of teaching one to fish as opposed to just feeding them. When we seek ways to generate income on an ongoing basis as opposed to seeking a one-time financial gain, we are that much closer to being free.

"Come, follow me," Jesus said, "and I will send you out to fish for people." Matthew 4:19

May 4

"Hardships often prepare ordinary people for an extraordinary destiny." ***C.S. Lewis***

When things get tough, it can be difficult to keep in mind that the hardships won't last, and that once they are over, there will be a valuable lesson that will serve you going forward.

"I consider that our present sufferings are not worth comparing with the glory that will be revealed in us."
Romans 8:18

May 5

"Don't count the days, make the days count."
Muhammad Ali

When you rise each morning, make every effort to be as productive as possible. If you identify your priorities, and remain focused on them throughout the day, when your day has ended, and you lay your head on your pillow at night, you will be proud of the contribution that you made that day.

"their work will be shown for what it is, because the Day will bring it to light. It will be revealed with fire, and the fire will test the quality of each person's work."
1 Corinthians 3:13

May 6

"Be the change you want to see in the world."
Mahatma Gandhi

Be cautious not to demand or require things from someone else, that you yourself are not able to deliver on.

"Join together in following my example, brothers and sisters, and just as you have us as a model, keep your eyes on those who live as we do." Philippians 3:17

May 7

"Being challenged in life is inevitable, being defeated is optional." ***Roger Crawford***

Challenge is necessary in order for us to grow. They key is not only to remember that you will get through them, but to know that you can.

"For the Lord your God is the one who goes with you to fight for you against your enemies to give you victory." Deuteronomy 20:4

May 8

"Hope and fear cannot occupy the same space, invite one to stay," ***Maya Angelou***

When we have hope, possibility is present, and this allows the space for miracles to happen.

"But I did not believe these things until I came and saw with my own eyes. Indeed, not even half was told me; in wisdom and wealth you have far exceeded the report I heard." 1 Kings 10:7

May 9

"Laughter is timeless, imagination has no age, and dreams are forever." ***Walt Disney***

If you are not spending some part of your day laughing, you are missing one of the most important ingredients of a balanced life.

"He will yet fill your mouth with laughter and your lips with shouts of joy." Job 8:21

May 10

"Never let pride be your guiding principle. Let your accomplishments speak for you."
Morgan Freeman

When you are a person of action, there is no need to be boast about the things that you've done. The difference that you make for people will be no mystery to the world.

"Do nothing out of selfish ambition or vain conceit. Rather, in humility value others above yourselves," Philippians 2:3

May 11

"Well done is better than well said."
Benjamin Franklin

Don't be that person who spends so much time talking that you never get anything done.

"Thus, by their fruit you will recognize them."
Matthew 7:20

May 12

"If you don't like something, change it. If you can't change it, change your attitude."
Maya Angelou

Complaining is an unproductive practice that harvests no results whatsoever. Shifting the results that you are seeing in your life lies in your ability to take action.

"to be made new in the attitude of your minds;"
Ephesians 4:23

May 13

“Imagination is more important than knowledge.”
Albert Einstein

Our imagination is the place of origin of the realities in our lives. It all starts with a thought.

"I pray that the eyes of your heart may be enlightened in order that you may know the hope to which he has called you, the riches of his glorious inheritance in his holy people," Ephesians 1:18

May 14

"What is now proven was once only imagined."
William Blake

When we become disciplined enough to visualize what we want, we are then able to create a future for ourselves.

"For no word from God will ever fail." Luke 1:37

May 15

"The real measure of your wealth is how much you'd be worth if you lost all your money."
Unknown

You can have all the money and material possessions in the world and still be bankrupt internally.

"Those who trust in their riches will fall, but the righteous will thrive like a green leaf." Proverbs 11:28

May 16

"Never let your situations or circumstances change you or define you." ***Loni Mendez***

"but those who hope in the Lord will renew their strength. They will soar on wings like eagles; they will run and not grow weary, they will walk and not be faint."
Isaiah 40:31

May 17

"Not all of us can do great things, but we can do small things with great love." ***Mother Teresa***

When it comes to helping people, little things make a big difference. So don't hesitate to do what you can, even if you'd like to do more but aren't able to. The love behind the intention counts more.

"Do everything in love." 1 Corinthians 16:14

May 18

"My greatest asset is that I am constantly changing." ***Jane Fonda***

Change is inevitable. Therefore, it would serve us to embrace it.

"Listen, I tell you a mystery: We will not all sleep, but we will all be changed—" 1 Corinthians 15:51

May 19

"The ladder of success is never crowded at the top." ***Unknown***

Not everyone is willing to expend the blood, sweat and tears that it takes to get to the top. Therefore, the road to success is not as popular as the path to mediocrity.

"The plans of the diligent lead to profit as surely as haste leads to poverty." Proverbs 21:5

May 20

"What you receive is directly connected to what you believe." ***Joel Osteen***

Once you truly understand the power that God gave us, and you are able to stand if faith for the things that you really want, you can literally create the life that you want rather than living your life by default.

"If you believe, you will receive whatever you ask for in prayer." Matthew 21:22

May 21

"Champions keep playing until they get it right."
Billie Jean King

Never forget that as long as you are living and breathing you can try again. It may take until your third of fourth attempt for you to reach a specific goal, but all that matters is that you eventually get it done. The amount of time it takes is unimportant.

"Let perseverance finish its work so that you may be mature and complete, not lacking anything." James 1:4

May 22

"If your dreams don't scare you, they are too small." ***Richard Branson***

When you set lofty goals and work towards accomplishing that next level, it can be scary. But there is no development in going for mediocrity. The stretch goals are the ones that help us to grow.

"May the favor of the Lord our God rest on us; establish the work of our hands for us— yes, establish the work of our hands." Psalms 90:17

May 23

"Faith is understanding that if things don't work out as planned, God will bring you through it and you will still be ok." ***Loni Mendez***

"so that your faith might not rest on human wisdom, but on God's power" 1 Corinthians 2:5

May 24

"I never question God's Divine Plan. There is a reason why God moves people out of your life; at the same token there will be people who will remain in your life in some capacity for the long haul, through many seasons...and then there are those who are in your life for a season and once that season is over it will no longer be in the cards for them to be part of your life." ***Loni Mendez***

"There is a time for everything, and a season for every activity under the heavens:" Ecclesiastes 3:1

May 25

" Knowledge is power, but execution trumps knowledge. "***Tony Robbins***

Knowing what to do has no impact on your life plans, it's the application of what you know that gets results.

"Those who work their land will have abundant food, but those who chase fantasies have no sense."
Proverbs 12:11

May 26

"Your limits are the lies your fears have told you."
Robin Sharma

Once we realize that our limits are self-imposed, we are armed with the knowledge that makes us unstoppable.

"Jesus looked at them and said, "With man this is impossible, but with God all things are possible."
Matthew 19:26

May 27

"One of the most important principles of success is developing the habit of going the extra mile."
Napoleon Hill

Always do more than that which is expected of you. It will pay off in the end.

"Now to him who is able to do immeasurably more than all we ask or imagine, according to his power that is at work within us," Ephesians 3:20

May 28

"The only time you should look down at someone is to help them up." ***Jessie Jackson***

Each of us will encounter misfortune in our lives at one point, it is a part of life that is unavoidable. When you see someone else who is going through tough times, remember do your best to imagine what it would be like for you if you were in their shoes.

"The righteous care about justice for the poor, but the wicked have no such concern." Proverbs 29:7

May 29

"If you are afraid of failure, you don't deserve to be successful." ***Charles Barkley***

When you don't allow failed plans or efforts to define you, it brings you one step closer to success. Acknowledge them for what they are, pray for strength, and start again.

"My flesh and my heart may fail, but God is the strength of my heart and my portion forever."
Psalms 73:26

May 30

"Every evening I turn my worries over to God.
He's going to be up all night anyway."
Mary C. Crowley

As someone who has trouble sleeping at night, I've learned to use breathing to relax me at night , and to ask God to take my worries off of my hands so that I can have a peaceful sleep.

*"Trust in the Lord with all your heart
and lean not on your own understanding;" Proverbs 3:5*

May 31

"He who is not courageous enough to take risks will accomplish nothing in life." ***Muhammad Ali***

The result of taking risks in life is uncertainty. But what people don't realize is that uncertainty is not necessarily a bad thing.

"Ship your grain across the sea; after many days you may receive a return." Ecclesiastes 11:1

June 1

"You don't need someone to complete you, you only need someone to accept you completely."
Unknown

When you meet that person who knows everything about you, and they still want to co-exist with you and create a future together, that is when you know that you've found the person you were meant to be with.

"He who finds a wife finds what is good and receives favor from the Lord." Proverbs 18:22

June 2

"It's not whether you get knocked down, it's whether you get up." ***Vince Lombardi***

To expect to move through life without challenges and setbacks would be unrealistic, the key is to learn how to be resilient in response to them.

"We are hard pressed on every side, but not crushed; perplexed, but not in despair;" 2 Corinthians 4:8

June 3

"There are no traffic jams on the extra mile."
Zig Ziglar

Going above and beyond is a hallmark of an extraordinary person. If you want to be successful in life, make a habit of doing more than what is expected.

"If anyone forces you to go one mile, go with them two miles." Matthew 5:41

June 4

"What others think about you is none of your business." ***Jack Canfield***

When you concern yourself with the opinions of others, it takes your focus away from living the purposeful life that God intended for you.

'Fools find no pleasure in understanding but delight in airing their own opinions." Proverbs 18:2

June 5

“"No one is useless in this world who lightens the burdens of another." ***Charles Dickens***

When you make the commitment to add value to everyone you come in contact with, there will be no question about the contribution you make to society.

“Carry each other’s burdens, and in this way you will fulfill the law of Christ.” Galatians 6:2

June 6

"When in doubt, tell the truth."
Mark Twain

Honesty will take you a long way in all of your relationships, both personal and business. It always wins over deceit.

"Therefore, rid yourselves of all malice and all deceit, hypocrisy, envy, and slander of every kind." 1 Peter 2:1

June 7

"Don't just aspire to make a living, aspire to make a difference." ***Denzel Washington***

When you are committed to being a contribution to people, you add another level of fulfillment to your own life.

"And if you do good to those who are good to you, what credit is that to you? Even sinners do that." Luke 6:33

June 8

"Normal is not something to aspire to, it's something to get away from." ***Jodie Foster***

The things about you that stand out are sometimes the things you dislike about yourself. Embrace those differences, they are what set you apart from others. Without them, the world would be full of clones, making it a pretty boring place.

"For just as each of us has one body with many members, and these members do not all have the same function,"
Romans 12:4

June 9

"You can't go back and change the beginning, but you can start where you are and change the ending." ***C.S. Lewis***

When you realize that all we have is right now, and that the past is gone and it cannot be changed, you are able to take the actions that will propel you forward in life.

"Joshua told the people, "Consecrate yourselves, for tomorrow the Lord will do amazing things among you." Joshua 3:5

June 10

"Do today what others won't so you can have tomorrow what others don't." ***Unknown***

Our feelings can be a hinderance to us if we are not careful. If we base what we do on how we feel, we would make very little progress in life. Learning to acknowledge our feelings and set them aside is a powerful tool that enables us to keep moving toward the things that we are striving for.

"Direct my footsteps according to your word; let no sin rule over me." Psalms 119:133

June 11

"We are born to be great, not to be perfect."
Unknown

It is ok to shoot for perfection as long as we realize that there is no such thing, and that none of us are perfect, because it powers us to do the absolute best that we can.

"As it is written: There is no one righteous, not even one;" Romans 3:10

June 12

"If you cannot find peace within yourself, you will never find it anywhere else." ***Marvin Gaye***

There is significant value in learning to be at peace with yourself and to not be envious of other people's good fortune.

"A heart at peace gives life to the body, but envy rots the bones." Proverbs 14:30

June 13

"Action is the foundational key to all success."
Pablo Picasso

When we decide to take a road trip, in order to reach our destination, we must get into the car and begin to drive. Life's accomplishments work in the same way, the only way to make progress is to get started.

"In the same way, faith by itself, if it is not accompanied by action, is dead." James 2:17

June 14

"The naked truth is always better than the best dressed lie." ***Unknown***

When you have to have a tough conversation with someone, or you have to tell them something they may not want to hear, look for ways to be eloquent and tactful without sugar-coating the message. Sometimes, it's not what you say that has the most impact, but how you say it.

"Then you will know the truth, and the truth will set you free." John 8:32

June 15

"Make your life a masterpiece; imagine no limitations on what you can be, have, or do."
Brian Tracy

While you have your health and vitality, make every effort to live a fulfilling life so that you have no regrets when you look back on your life after you've aged.

"I am the vine; you are the branches. If you remain in me and I in you, you will bear much fruit; apart from me you can do nothing." John 15:5

June 16

"Goals are dreams with a deadline."
Napoleon Hill

What I've found is that when I really want to take on a project, I have to put my stake in the ground by creating a date by which I will complete the project. With no deadline or anticipated completion date in sight, it will just be an ongoing conversation topic.

"In the same way, faith by itself, if it is not accompanied by action, is dead." James 2:17

June 17

"Humility is a flower which does not grow in everyone's garden." ***Aristotle***

It is more respectable to be modest than to be someone who constantly boasts about their accomplishments.

"Humble yourselves before the Lord, and he will lift you up." James 4:10

June 18

"There are two kinds of people in the world, people with reasons and people with results."
Unknown

The people you spend your time with have an effect on your view of life, and ultimately, on what you are able to accomplish. Surround yourself with those who are ambitious and are making an impact in the world, as opposed to those who are doing nothing.

"One who is slack in his work is brother to one who destroys." Proverbs 18:9

June 19

"If you ever find yourself in the wrong story, leave." ***Unknown***

Most of what goes on in our heads are stories that we've made up., and more often than not, these are stories with undesirable outcomes. Since they are made up by us anyway, why not make up some stories that have happy endings.

'If you remain in me and my words remain in you, ask whatever you wish, and it will be done for you." John 15:7

June 20

"People can't see your intentions, they can only see your actions." ***Unknown***

"We can listen to a person's words all day every day, but it's their actions that speak the truth about who they really are."

"Like clouds and wind without rain is one who boasts of gifts never given." Proverbs 25:14

June 21

"Education is not the learning of facts but the training of the mind to think."
Albert Einstein

Our minds are so powerful, and have the ability to process and retain a vast amount of knowledge. Yet, most people only a minute fraction of their mental capacity.

"let the wise listen and add to their learning, and let the discerning get guidance" Proverbs 1:5

June 22

"We don't need to explain our love. We only need to show it." ***Paulo Coelho***

Our love is evident in the way that we treat others. It will have a nurturing effect on them that needs no language.

"Love does not delight in evil but rejoices with the truth. It always protects, always trusts, always hopes, always perseveres." 1 Corinthians 13:6-7

June 23

"Service is the rent we pay for being,. It is the very purpose of life and not something you do in your spare time." ***Marion Wright Edelman***

Each and every one of us is here to change the world, one good deed, one act of kindness…one person at a time.

"Whoever is kind to the poor lends to the Lord, and he will reward them for what they have done." Proverbs 19:17

June 24

"If your actions inspire others to dream more, learn more, do more and become more, you are a leader." ***John Quincy Adams***

If you aspire to be a leader in this world, you must demonstrate an unwavering commit to motivating, inspiring and lifting people up.

"And let us consider how we may spur one another on toward love and good deeds" Hebrews 10:24

June 25

"Every day do something that will inch you closer to a better tomorrow." ***Doug Firebaugh***

Change and progress are incremental and do not happen overnight. But the little steps that you take each day will prove to make a monumental difference over time.

"Be wise in the way you act toward outsiders; make the most of every opportunity." Colossians 4:5

June 26

"The world is a book and those who do not travel read only one page." ***St. Augustine***

One of my true passions is traveling the world. I always say that God did not create this vast universe for us to hide in one tiny little corner all of our lives.

"By day the Lord went ahead of them in a pillar of cloud to guide them on their way and by night in a pillar of fire to give them light, so that they could travel by day or night." Exodus 13:21

June 27

"Learning to distance yourself from all the negativity is one of the greatest lessons to achieve inner peace." ***Roy T. Bennett***

When you make it clear through your actions that you do not participate in negative behaviors such as gossip or slander, you will become known for it and negative people will automatically take a detour past you to move on to someone whom they know will partake in their destructive behavior.

"Those who guard their mouths and their tongues keep themselves from calamity." Proverbs 21:23

June 28

"Our children can be our greatest teachers if we are humble enough to receive their lessons."
Bryant H. McGill

Children are such free beings that they believe they can do anything, they speak their mind with no reservation, and they love and forgive without hesitation. Although we are not conscious of it, as adults, it is our conditioning that slowly diminishes that freedom during their formative years.

"Whoever welcomes one of these little children in my name welcomes me; and whoever welcomes me does not welcome me but the one who sent me." Mark 9:37

June 29

"Tranquility is not weakness; from tranquility emerges power and strength." ***C. Joybell C.***

Sometimes doing or saying less can make the most powerful statement. Silent prayer is the most effective approach.

"I pray that out of his glorious riches he may strengthen you with power through his Spirit in your inner being,"
Ephesians 3:16

June 30

"Success is the sum of small efforts, repeated day in and day out." ***Robert J. Collier***

The way that you spend your time each day should reflect the things that are most important to you in life. Even a little progress each day toward that ultimate goal, is better than being stuck in one place for an extended period of time.

"The Lord our God said to us at Horeb, "You have stayed long enough at this mountain." Deuteronomy 1:6

July 1

"There's no real ending. It's just the place where you stop the story." ***Frank Herbert***

Our stay here on this earth is temporary, but there is a place within each of us, a place that encompasses both our spirit and our soul, that lives on beyond the temporal.

"The world and its desires pass away, but whoever does the will of God lives forever." 1 John 2:17

July 2

"People of excellence go the extra mile to do what's right." ***Joel Osteen***

It has been proven that when you do more than what is required with no expectation of a return on your investment, the score is eventually evened and you are re-paid tenfold.

"And they exceeded our expectations: They gave themselves first of all to the Lord, and then by the will of God also to us." 2 Corinthians 8:5

July 3

"In order to experience the extraordinary, you must be willing to let go of the mediocre."
Loni Mendez

"Not that I have already obtained all this, or have already arrived at my goal, but I press on to take hold of that for which Christ Jesus took hold of me." Philippians 3:12

July 4

"Make use of time, let not advantage slip."
William Shakespeare

Time management is imperative when you are up to big things. When you rise each morning, make every effort to plan your time so that it is used wisely.

"But everything should be done in a fitting and orderly way." 1 Corinthians 14:40

July 5

"If you are not willing to learn, no one can help you. If you are determined to learn, no one can stop you." ***Zig Ziglar***

Ongoing growth and development is non-negotiable for living a life of purpose and fulfillment.

"The righteous will flourish like a palm tree, they will grow like a cedar of Lebanon;" Psalms 92:12

July 6

"The keys to writing your own ticket in life involve:

* trusting God
* spending time in silence/solitude
* raising your standards
* setting goals; and
* doing the work

At the end of the day...the reality is that no cavalry is coming....you're it! AND, each and every one of us has what it takes to achieve our goals!"

Loni Mendez

"But as for you, be strong and do not give up, for your work will be rewarded." 2 Chronicles 15:7

July 7

"The difference between skill and talent is: talent is given to us by God; whereas, skill is developed by us." ***Will Smith***

When we combine the talents that God has gifted us and the skills that we have developed through years of life experience, we become unstoppable.

"For this reason I remind you to fan into flame the gift of God, which is in you through the laying on of my hands." 2 Timothy 1:6

July 8

"Great things take time to manifest! It is impossible to rush extraordinary outcomes."
Loni Mendez

"But if we hope for what we do not yet have, we wait for it patiently." Romans 8:25

July 9

"Inner peace begins the moment you choose not to let another person or event control your emotions." ***Pema Chodron***

We can't always control outside forces that impact our lives, and we certainly cannot control other people, but what we can control is ourselves. When we are going through tough times, we have the power within ourselves to decide who we are going to be in response to our circumstances.

"Lord, who may dwell in your sacred tent? Who may live on your holy mountain? The one whose walk is blameless, who does what is righteous," Psalms 15:1-2

July 10

"True friendship is a plant of slow growth."
George Washington

Sometimes you meet people with whom you get along well, and you quickly discover that you have many things in common. This is a great beginning, but building a true friendship or partnership takes time. It takes time to build trust and to develop that connection into something that is sustainable.

"How good and pleasant it is when God's people live together in unity!" Psalms 133:1

July 11

"Preparedness makes us powerful."
Hermann Goering

We never know when an opportunity might be presented to us without warning. Therefore, it would serve us well to be prepared just in case.

"He who gathers crops in summer is a prudent son, but he who sleeps during harvest is a disgraceful son."
Proverbs 10:5

July 12

"Growth is the only evidence of life."
John Henry Newman

A fulfilling life is one in which we challenge ourselves to learn and experience new things.

"I said to myself, "Look, I have increased in wisdom more than anyone who has ruled over Jerusalem before me; I have experienced much of wisdom and knowledge."
Ecclesiastes 1:16

July 13

"It's not always that we need to do more but rather that we need to focus on less."
Nathan W. Morris

Our ability to focus is what drives results when it comes to the successful completion of the goals that we set out to achieve.

"Watch your life and doctrine closely. Persevere in them, because if you do, you will save both yourself and your hearers." 1 Timothy 4:16

July 14

"We make a living by what we get. We make a life by what we give." ***Winston S. Churchill***

Never underestimate the power of giving. If you don't have the financial means to donate money, consider that you can donate services that entail the use of your gifts and talents, or you can donate your time.

"For if the willingness is there, the gift is acceptable according to what one has, not according to what one does not have." 2 Corinthians 8:12

July 15

"Do your duty and a little more, and the future will take care of itself." ***Andrew Carnegie***

Always be willing to contribute more than what is expected. If you do not seek a return for going that extra mile, in the long run you will be rewarded.

"Now to him who is able to do immeasurably more than all we ask or imagine, according to his power that is at work within us," Ephesians 3:20

July 16

"The highest rung of what's possible is far beyond the world you could see." ***From the book, Born A Crime, by Trevor Noah***

Sometimes, striving for success might include aiming for something that you can't see or didn't even know existed.

"However, as it is written: "What no eye has seen, what no ear has heard, and what no human mind has conceived" — the things God has prepared for those who love him—" 1 Corinthians 2:9

July 17

"Change is inevitable. Growth is optional."
John C. Maxwell

Our ability to adapt to change is directly related to the level of success that we can achieve.

"I am not saying this because I am in need, for I have learned to be content whatever the circumstances. 12 I know what it is to be in need, and I know what it is to have plenty. I have learned the secret of being content in any and every situation, whether well fed or hungry, whether living in plenty or in want." Ephesians 4:11-12

July 18

"Nature is pleased with simplicity."
Isaac Newton

When all else fails, aim to keep it simple. "Simple" can be understood and comprehended by human beings from all walks of life.

"For God is not a God of disorder but of peace—as in all the congregations of the Lord's people."
1 Corinthians 14:33

July 19

"Anything can be achieved with a good, healthy dose of courage." ***Viola Davis***

Fear stops us from trying; Courage gives us the power to move forward.

"Even though I walk through the darkest valley, I will fear no evil, for you are with me; your rod and your staff, they comfort me." Psalms 23:4

July 20

"You are not given a dream unless you have the capacity to fulfill it." ***Jack Canfield***

Those deep desires that linger on until we do something about them exist for a reason. They are the calls to action that send us out into the world to fulfill on the purpose that God has chosen us for.

"For many are invited, but few are chosen."
Matthew 22:14

July 21

"Never let someone else's opinion of you determine your value." ***Unknown***

People will always have their opinions, but we are not in the business of explaining ourselves or convincing anyone of anything. However, your actions speak louder than any explanation you could ever give.

'For it is God's will that by doing good you should silence the ignorant talk of foolish people." 1 Peter 2:15

July 22

"Your whole life is a manifestation of the thoughts that go on in your head."
Lisa Nicols

While we are unable to control our thoughts, with practice, we can learn to redirect them.

"Do not conform to the pattern of this world, but be transformed by the renewing of your mind. Then you will be able to test and approve what God's will is—his good, pleasing and perfect will." Romans 12:2

July 23

"Successful people live where the opportunities are, which is outside their comfort zone."
Unknown

To experience new things and to reach new levels of success, we must abandon comfort.

"Call to me and I will answer you and tell you great and unsearchable things you do not know.' Jeremiah 33:3

July 24

"Some people are so poor that all they have is money." ***Christylezz***

Financial wealth is not the only form of wealth. You can have no money in your bank account and still be wealthier than the richest people in the world.

"Better a little with the fear of the Lord than great wealth with turmoil." Proverbs 15:16

July 25

"True nobility is not about being better than anybody else, it's about being better than you used to be." ***Wayne Dyer***

A good way to avoid comparing yourself to others is to focus on the progress that you've made, or that you're currently making in your own life. Everyone is on a unique path, designed specifically for their journey according to God's will.

"equip you with everything good for doing his will, and may he work in us what is pleasing to him, through Jesus Christ, to whom be glory for ever and ever. Amen."
Hebrews 13:21

July 26

"The key is not to prioritize what's on your schedule, but to schedule your priorities."
Stephen Covey

Just as God's creations operate on a schedule, high performers understand that accomplishing great things starts with your schedule.

"He made the moon to mark the seasons, and the sun knows when to go down." Psalms 104:19

July 27

"You don't have to be great to start, but you have to start to be great." ***Zig Ziglar***

When you find yourself procrastinating, remember how it felt when you took the first action the last time? Ask God for a little push toward making that initial step. All you need is that first action to trigger the momentum that is required to get whatever it is done.

"for it is God who works in you to will and to act in order to fulfill his good purpose." Philippians 2:13

July 28

"To the one who has faith no explanation is necessary. To the one without faith no explanation is possible." ***Thomas Aquinas***

If you don't believe, no one can convince you of what you are capable of.

"Truly I tell you, if anyone says to this mountain, 'Go, throw yourself into the sea,' and does not doubt in their heart but believes that what they say will happen, it will be done for them." Mark 11:23

July 29

"One of the greatest regrets in life is being what others would want you to be, rather than being yourself." ***Shannon L. Alder***

Never give up on the vision for your life to please another person. It's not like you can live out their dreams in this life, and yours in the next. The reality is, we only have this one life.

"What good is it for someone to gain the whole world, and yet lose or forfeit their very self?" Luke 9:25

July 30

"If you are going to doubt something, doubt your limits." ***Unknown***

Doubt lives in the same habitat as fear, and either of them can attach themselves to your goals and aspirations. You have the power to leave them both behind, you just need to believe that you can.

"But when you ask, you must believe and not doubt, because the one who doubts is like a wave of the sea, blown and tossed by the wind." James 1:6

July 31

"Everything you do is triggered by an emotion of either desire or fear." ***Brian Tracy***

Desire is not the only force that drives people to success. There are some very successful people in the world who have been driven to success by the fear of something that they wanted to avoid at all cost.

"Stand firm, and you will win life." Luke 21:19

August 1

"The past does not equal the future, unless you live there." ***Tony Robbins***

If you are looking to move forward, don't make space in your luggage for your past.

*"Create in me a pure heart, O God,
and renew a steadfast spirit within me." Psalms 51:10*

August 2

"Happiness is the greatest form of health."
Dalai Lama

When you learn how to create happiness from within yourself, you have reached a major milestone that will serve you for the remainder of your life.

"A cheerful heart is good medicine, but a crushed spirit dries up the bones." Proverbs 17:22

August 3

"Whether you think you can, or you think you can't – you're right." ***Henry Ford***

The mind is so powerful that it literally controls our destiny. Therefore, it would serve us to train our minds to focus on the best possible outcome in all situations.

"Finally, brothers and sisters, whatever is true, whatever is noble, whatever is right, whatever is pure, whatever is lovely, whatever is admirable—if anything is excellent or praiseworthy—think about such things." Philippians 4:8

August 4

"Discipline is the bridge between goals and accomplishment." ***Jim Rohn***

So many alleged goals remain unaccomplished in spite of their creators having most of the fundamental tools to make them a reality. If they are not disciplined enough to take the action, all they really have is a dream.

"No discipline seems pleasant at the time, but painful. Later on, however, it produces a harvest of righteousness and peace for those who have been trained by it." Hebrews 12:11

August 5

"Education is the most powerful weapon which you can used to change the world."
Nelson Mandela

The best thing that you can do for yourself is to continue to learn and grow for as long as you live. There are countless ways that we can educate ourselves, a formal institution is only one option.

"Wisdom makes one wise person more powerful than ten rulers in a city." Ecclesiastes 7:19

August 6

"When someone shows you who they are the first time, believe them." ***Maya Angelou***

If you pay close attention, a person's actions and behavior are all you need to distinguish who they really are. Once you learn who they are, if you feel that they are not someone who you'd like to remain a part of your life, do not allow denial to creep in, causing you to make an exception. Later on down the road, your first instinct will prove to have been accurate.

"and many false prophets will appear and deceive many people." Matthew 24:11

August 7

"You must gain control over your money, or the lack of it will forever control you."
Dave Ramsey

It is not uncommon for people to be stopped when it comes to their finances. Many of us have grown up without having been educated about money. But now that we are adults, we can educate ourselves and learn to take control of our financial situation. Financial education can change your life and free you from that familiar stigma that exists around money.

"Keep your lives free from the love of money and be content with what you have, because God has said, "Never will I leave you; never will I forsake you." Hebrews 13:5

August 8

"Don't cry because it's over. Smile because it happened." ***Unknown***

Experiencing hurtful events and loss are a part of life and are unavoidable. We've all been in that place where we've had to leave someone that we love behind. Perhaps it was a relationship that wasn't working. Rather than allowing the memory to depress you, try focusing on and appreciating the value that the relationship brought to your life.

"Blessed are those who mourn, for they will be comforted." Matthew 5:4

August 9

"Honesty is the first chapter in the book of wisdom." ***Thomas Jefferson***

When dealing with conflict, it makes sense to be straightforward with people so that you are able to come to an agreement with them. A powerful practice is to start with a buffer by acknowledging your concern for how the conversation might go and your desire to work it out in advance.

"Do not lie to each other, since you have taken off your old self with its practices" Colossians 3:9

August 10

"If you want to fly give up everything that weighs you down." ***Unknown***

If you have people in your life who are takers that do not reciprocate, consider minimizing the time that you spend with them. Even if it's not an equal exchange, two parties in a friendship, relationship or partnership should be contributing to each other in lieu of one party weighing the other down.

"Do not lie to each other, since you have taken off your old self with its practices" Luke 6:31

August 11

"The only real mistake is the one from which we learn nothing." ***Henry Ford***

Mistakes are part of our lives for a reason. The key is to avoid making the same mistake over and over again.

"We all stumble in many ways." James 3:2a

August 12

"Who you are tomorrow begins with what you do today." ***Tim Fargo***

Now is the perfect time to start working toward that vision you have for your future. The longer you take to get started, the longer it will take for you to get there.

"Then they asked him, "What must we do to do the works God requires?" John 6:28

August 13

"At every moment we have the power to choose the meaning we give things that happen in our lives." ***Loni Mendez***

"Undoubtedly there are all sorts of languages in the world, yet none of them is without meaning."
1 Corinthians 14:10

August 14

"Nothing is certain, because anything is possible!"
Loni Mendez

"I know that you can do all things; no purpose of yours can be thwarted." Job 42:2

August 15

"Simplicity is the ultimate sophistication."
Leonardo da Vinci

When we keep things simple, we make life easy for ourselves and the people we live and work with.

"The law of the Lord is perfect, refreshing the soul. The statutes of the Lord are trustworthy, making wise the simple." Psalms 19:7

August 16

"There is no end to the good you can do if you don't care who gets the credit." ***Colin Powell***

True service is when you do things for others without seeking recognition and with no concern for whether people know about what you've done.

"And if you lend to those from whom you expect repayment, what credit is that to you? Even sinners lend to sinners, expecting to be repaid in full." Luke 6:34

August 17

"The ladder of success is best climbed by stepping on the wings of opportunity." ***Ayn Rand***

When opportunities come along in life, if you've prepared yourself, you will be able identify and take advantage of them without hesitation.

'Therefore, as we have opportunity, let us do good to all people, especially to those who belong to the family of believers." Galatians 6:10

August 18

"When you're up to big things, and you are doing God's work, small problems disappear."
Loni Mendez

"The Lord is good, a refuge in times of trouble. He cares for those who trust in him," Nahum 1:7

August 19

"The secret of your success is determined by your daily agenda." ***John Maxwell***

How you spend your time each day should ultimately bring you closer to meeting your goals and aspirations.

"Joseph is a fruitful vine, a fruitful vine near a spring, whose branches climb over a wall." Genesis 49:22

August 20

"The only place where success comes before work is in the dictionary." ***Vidal Sassoon***

Anything worth having in life is going to cost you time, effort and hard work at the very least.

'For even when we were with you, we gave you this rule: "The one who is unwilling to work shall not eat." 2 Thessalonians 3:10

August 21

"Confidence is contagious. So is lack of confidence." ***Vince Lombardi***

When you surround yourself with people who are doing great things, you will start to see the great things that you, yourself are capable of doing.

"So do not throw away your confidence; it will be richly rewarded." Hebrews 10:35

August 22

"We work to earn our leisure." ***Aristotle***

There is something about putting in a hard day's work that makes downtime so much more enjoyable.

"Come to me, all you who are weary and burdened, and I will give you rest." Matthew 11:28

August 23

"Doing what you love is the cornerstone of having abundance in your life." ***Wayne Dyer***

When you do what you love for a living, success is inevitable. Our passions point us in the direction in which God wants us to focus our efforts.

"Therefore, my dear brothers and sisters, stand firm. Let nothing move you. Always give yourselves fully to the work of the Lord, because you know that your labor in the Lord is not in vain." 1 Corinthians 15:58

August 24

"Believe you can and you're halfway there."
Theodore Roosevelt

A major factor in attaining success is mindset. Therefore, conditioning your mind for high performance and achievement with a positive attitude should be a part of your daily routine.

"With joy you will draw water from the wells of salvation."
Isaiah 12:3

August 25

"If you cannot do great things, do small things in a great way." ***Napoleon Hill***

When you take on making a difference in the world, don't worry about how big or small your contribution is, just do the absolute best job you can in whatever role you decide to play in making the world a better place.

"God will repay each person according to what they have done" *Romans 2:6*

August 26

"If somebody offers you an amazing opportunity but you are not sure you can do it, say yes, then figure out how to do it later." ***Richard Branson***

Never underestimate what you are capable of. Accepting those stretch assignments are a sure way of making sure that you are developing your skills. Trust that God will provide you with what you need to make it happen.

"If any of you lacks wisdom, you should ask God, who gives generously to all without finding fault, and it will be given to you." James 1:5

August 27

"Well done is better than well said."
Benjamin Franklin

Don't be that person who talks a good game but gets nothing done. Be the person who did the work and completed the task.

"I have fought the good fight, I have finished the race, I have kept the faith." 2 Timothy 4:7

August 28

"The secret of getting ahead is getting started."
Mark Twain

As hard as that first step might be to getting something done, once you take it the momentum to complete the past will follow.

"They charge like warriors; they scale walls like soldiers. They all march in line, not swerving from their course." Joel 2:7

August 29

"Many of life's failures are people who did not realize how close they were to success when they gave up." ***Thomas Edison***

When failure is not an option, you will keep going until you go all the way.

"Stand firm, and you will win life." Luke 21:19

August 30

"Real knowledge is to know the extent of one's ignorance." ***Confucius***

Even though I am a person who loves talking, I am smart enough not to discuss topics with which I am unfamiliar. I am the first one to acknowledge when I don't know about a particular subject, and turn the floor over to those who can speak intelligently about that topic.

"The heart of the righteous weighs its answers, but the mouth of the wicked gushes evil." Proverbs 15:28

August 31

"Happiness is not a goal, it's a by-product of a life well lived." ***Eleanor Roosevelt***

When you discover the beauty of living life on purpose, you will learn that happiness and contentment automatically become part of the equation.

"But godliness with contentment is great gain."
1 Timothy 6:6

September 1

"How people treat you is their karma, how you react is yours." ***Wayne Dyer***

In life, people will do things that affect you, and that may be hurtful. Take these actions with a grain of salt, practice forgiveness and challenge yourself to be the bigger person. It's not always easy to take the high road, but it's always worth it.

"Do not seek revenge or bear a grudge against anyone among your people, but love your neighbor as yourself."
Leviticus 19:18

September 2

"If you look at what you have in life, you will always have more. If you look at what you don't have in life, you'll never have enough." ***Oprah Winfrey***

Viewing the glass as half full has a significant impact on what you are able to accomplish. Being grateful for the blessing of having our basic needs met creates the space for us to receive more blessings. Context is decisive.

"But if we have food and clothing, we will be content with that." 1 Timothy 6:8

September 3

"Nothing is impossible. The word itself says I'm Possible." ***Audrey Hepburn***

Your belief in what you can achieve is the fuel that powers your actions which dictate the final outcome.

"Jesus looked at them and said, "With man this is impossible, but not with God; all things are possible with God." Mark 10:27

September 4

"You can give without loving, but you cannot love without giving." ***Amy Carmichael***

When we understand God's command for us to love one another, giving of ourselves becomes second nature.

"A new command I give you: Love one another. As I have loved you, so you must love one another." John 13:34

September 5

"Your past doesn't define you, it prepares you."
Darren Hardy

Learning to let go of the past is prudent in our quest for greatness. It involves embracing the lessons that our past has taught us and the application of what we've learned as we create our futures.

"Brothers and sisters, I do not consider myself yet to have taken hold of it. But one thing I do: Forgetting what is behind and straining toward what is ahead,"
Philippians 3:13

September 6

"We cannot change anything unless we accept it."
Carl Jung

In order to make improvements we must acknowledge that there has been a breakdown in performance, identify what was missing, and incorporate those findings into our revised plan of action.

"Show me your ways, Lord, teach me your paths."
Psalms 25:4

September 7

"The more you like yourself the less you are like anyone else, which makes you unique."
Walt Disney

Loving yourself is accompanied by a wisdom and understanding that results in a love for life.

"The one who gets wisdom loves life;
the one who cherishes understanding will soon prosper."
Proverbs 19:8

September 8

"We accept the love we think we deserve."
Stephen Chbosky

In God's eyes we are all His children, and are deserving of His love.

"See what great love the Father has lavished on us, that we should be called children of God! And that is what we are! " 1 John 3:1

September 9

"The measure of a man is what he does with power." ***Plato***

When you have power there is no need for force. A powerful person who recognizes this, and who uses kindness and understanding to make their decisions is a virtuous person.

"He upholds the cause of the oppressed and gives food to the hungry. The Lord sets prisoners free," Psalms 146:7

September 10

"Expect the best and people will rise to the occasion." ***James Kerr***

Your expectations have a direct impact on how people respond to you.

"May he send you help from the sanctuary and grant you support from Zion." *Psalms 20:2*

September 11

"It's amazing how life will organize around the standards you set for yourself."
Darren Hardy

When you set the bar for how you are going to live, who you are going to be, and the kind of people you are going to surround yourself with, the elements that support those standards arrange themselves accordingly.

"for kings and all those in authority, that we may live peaceful and quiet lives in all godliness and holiness."
1 Timothy 2:2

September 12

"Acknowledging the good that you already have in your life is the foundation for all abundance."
Eckert Tolle

When we develop the practice of appreciating all the things in our lives that we have to be grateful for, we open new doors in terms of what is available to us.

"then your barns will be filled to overflowing, and your vats will brim over with new wine." Proverbs 3:10

September 13

"Music is a higher revelation than all wisdom and philosophy." ***Ludwig Van Beethoven***

God gave us the gift of music for many reasons: it comforts us, it makes us happy, but most of all, it provides us with another way to express our love for Him and to Him.

"Is anyone among you in trouble? Let them pray. Is anyone happy? Let them sing songs of praise." James 5:13

September 14

"Mastering others is strength, mastering yourself is true power." ***Lao Tzu***

There is no substitute for discipline, for it is one of the fundamental elements of achievement. Commit to developing yourself in that area, and you cannot go wrong.

"Nevertheless, the righteous will hold to their ways, and those with clean hands will grow stronger." Job 17:9

September 15

"When the power of love overcomes the love of power, the world will know peace." ***Jimi Hendrix***

Power can be the tool that helps us overcome many of the world's greatest challenges. But if it is coupled with greed and selfishness, it can destroy an entire nation.

"I have given you authority to trample on snakes and scorpions and to overcome all the power of the enemy; nothing will harm you." Luke 10:19

September 16

"The secret to having it all is believing you already do." ***Unknown***

Life is like an empty canvas, and we are the artists. We have been blessed with all of the tools that we need to create whatever we want in our lives. However, many are unaware of what we, as God's children, are capable of.

"And my God will meet all your needs according to the riches of his glory in Christ Jesus." Philippians 4:19

September 17

"The greatest force in the world today is the power of God as it works through man."
Thomas S. Monson

The next time you reach a major goal, and you are wondering how you were able accomplish something so vast, consider God orders our steps to support us in expediting His divine plan.

"I will instruct you and teach you in the way you should go; I will counsel you with my loving eye on you."
Psalms 32:8

September 18

"Don't follow your dreams. Chase them down with aggressive pursuit." ***Daren Hardy***

"Be the person who spends your life transforming your dreams into realities, in lieu of the person who sits on them and wonders if they could ever become more than just dreams.

"Make every effort to enter through the narrow door, because many, I tell you, will try to enter and will not be able to." Luke 13:24

September 19

"Leadership is the power of one harnessing the power of many." ***John Maxwell***

When God has gifted you with charisma, and the ability to influence people, you are summoned with using those gifts to create disciples who will spread love and do good things in the world.

"Therefore go and make disciples of all nations, baptizing them in the name of the Father and of the Son and of the Holy Spirit," Matthew 28:19

September 20

"It's never too late to be who you might have been." ***George Elliot***

Our experiences teach us about life and prepare us for the work that we have been put on this earth to do. By the time we have been shaped by these experiences, youth may no longer be on our side. In spite of this, it is never too late to put what we've learned to good use.

"But the plans of the Lord stand firm forever, the purposes of his heart through all generations." Psalms 33:11

September 21

"If you're brave enough to start, you're strong enough to finish." ***Gary Ryan Blair***

When you take that first step, you are already way ahead of those who are still struggling to get started.

"The Lord makes firm the steps of the one who delights in him;" Psalms 37:23

September 22

"The secret of happiness, you see, is not found in seeking more, but in developing the capacity to enjoy less." ***Socrates***

The more we are able to create our own happiness, independent of the need for material things, the richer our experience of life will ultimately be.

"Keep your lives free from the love of money and be content with what you have" Hebrews 13:5

September 23

"Injustice anywhere is a threat to justice everywhere." ***Dr. Martin Luther King, Jr.***

If you are tempted to turn the other cheek when you witness injustice in the world, remember that in reality we are all one.

"Let the peace of Christ rule in your hearts, since as members of one body you were called to peace. And be thankful." Colossians 3:15

September 24

"Sometimes you have to go through everything, to get to nothing, so that you can create something."
Loni Mendez

"Therefore, if anyone is in Christ, the new creation has come: The old has gone, the new is here!"
2 Corinthians 5:17

September 25

"An inch of movement will bring you closer to your goals than a mile of intention."
Steve Maraboli

We all mean to get around to facing our giants, taking on the things in our lives that mean so much to us. But keep in mind that nothing can be accomplished with mere intention.

"Dear children, let us not love with words or speech but with actions and in truth." 1 John 3:18

September 26

"Set peace of mind as your highest goal, then organize your life around it." ***Brian Tracy***

Peace of mind should be at the foundation of all your efforts. Without it, you will not be able to focus, nor will you be productive.

"the Lord turn his face toward you and give you peace."
Numbers 6:26

September 27

"Kindness in words creates confidence.
Kindness in thinking creates profoundness.
Kindness in giving creates love." ***Tao Tzu***

Being kind to others costs us absolutely nothing, and has an impact on the world that is so great it cannot be measured.

"Anxiety weighs down the heart, but a kind word cheers it up." Proverbs 12:25

September 28

"Responsibilities gravitate to the person who shoulders them." ***Tom Stoppard***

Have you ever wondered why you were appointed to handle the greatest, most monumental tasks? Consider that it is because you are the one who was chosen for others to lean on in their time of need.

"Anyone who does not provide for their relatives, and especially for their own household, has denied the faith and is worse than an unbeliever." 1 Timothy 5:8

September 29

"If you don't fail, you're not even trying."
Denzel Washington

There is no such thing as instant success. Success is constructed on the back of many failures.

"Consider it pure joy, my brothers and sisters, whenever you face trials of many kinds," James 1:2

September 30

"Life isn't about waiting for the storm to pass, it's about learning to dance in the rain." ***Unknown***

In the midst of a breakdown, you've got to be willing to celebrate the victory that has not yet been won with the certainty that it is soon to come.

"for everyone born of God overcomes the world. This is the victory that has overcome the world, even our faith."
1 John 5:4

October 1

"To love is to recognize yourself in another."
Eckert Tolle

After many decades of living among fellow human beings, I've found that it really isn't difficult to relate to people. While we are each experiencing our own journey, we are all dealing with similar challenges…the challenges of life.

"And over all these virtues put on love, which binds them all together in perfect unity." Colossians 3:14

October 2

"Truth never damages a cause that is just,"
Mahatma Gandhi

Even if it is difficult to tell the truth, the important people in your life will appreciate your honesty.

The lips of the righteous know what finds favor, but the mouth of the wicked only what is perverse."
Proverbs 10:32

October 3

"A good plan today is better than a perfect plan tomorrow." G***eorge Patton***

There is no better time than now for you to take action, and every action you take toward your goals and dreams counts.

"Do not boast about tomorrow, for you do not know what a day may bring." Proverbs 27:1

October 4

"Nothing will work unless you do."
Maya Angelou

When you are willing to put in the hard work required to have what you want, you are far more appreciative of those things when it all pays off.

"Diligent hands will rule, but laziness ends in forced labor." Proverbs 12:24

October 5

"Everything will be OK in the end. If it's not OK then it's not the end." ***Unknown***

When you are up against obstacles in life, just take a moment to think back on how God carried you through every single one of your past challenges. If He hadn't, you wouldn't be where you are right now.

"Put on the full armor of God, so that you can take your stand against the devil's schemes." Ephesians 6:11

October 6

"Excellence is not a skill, it is an attitude."
Ralph Marston

When you take on doing and being your absolute best, the end result is excellence.

"For this very reason, make every effort to add to your faith goodness; and to goodness, knowledge;" 2 Peter 1:5

October 7

"Responsibility is the price of greatness."
Winston Churchill

When you are not afraid to be a light of hope for the world, the world responds by seeking your leadership

"The elders who direct the affairs of the church well are worthy of double honor, especially those whose work is preaching and teaching." 1 Timothy 5:17

October 8

"Excellence is the gradual result of always striving to do better." ***Pat Riley***

When you work diligently to produce quality results, you become known for doing good work, and your reputation speaks for itself.

"In everything set them an example by doing what is good. In your teaching show integrity, seriousness" Titus 2:7

October 9

"Conflict cannot survive without your participation." ***Wayne Dyer***

When you are in disagreement with someone, and they are unwilling to have a constructive conversation, it may serve you better to calmly ask to revisit the matter at another time and stop talking, rather than stir up more conflict.

"A gentle answer turns away wrath,
but a harsh word stirs up anger." Proverbs 15:1

October 10

"Never give up on something that you can't go a day without thinking about." ***Winston Churchill***

Each of us have a job to do in life. When we listen to our inner spirit, it provides us with direction. The work that is meant for you will continue to be on your heart, and will most likely involve the talents that God gifted you with. This is how you will be able to identify your calling.

"I wish that all of you were as I am. But each of you has your own gift from God; one has this gift, another has that." 1 Corinthians 7:7

October 11

"Tough times never last, but tough people do."
Robert H. Schuller

Life's challenges have a shelf life, and when they reach their end, you will emerge better and stronger than you were before they surfaced.

"He gives strength to the weary and increases the power of the weak." Isaiah 40:29

October 12

"Perhaps the grass always seems greener on the other side because it's fake." ***Unknown***

Comparing yourself to others is a sure way to stunt your own growth. Each of us is on a different journey, traveling at different paces. Be mindful of your own journey and your own pace, and no one else's.

"You must each accept the responsibilities that are yours." Galatians 6:5

October 13

"Our greatest weakness lies in giving up."
Thomas Edison

When we give up on our goals and dreams, we simultaneously relinquish the strength and power that is rightfully ours.

"If you falter in a time of trouble, how small is your strength!" Proverbs 24:10

October 14

"The purpose of life is to contribute in some way to making things better."
Robert F. Kennedy

Being a contribution to our fellow human beings is our duty and our responsibility.

"Share with the Lord's people who are in need. Practice hospitality." Romans 12:13

October 15

"We are not human beings having a spiritual experience, we are spiritual beings having a human experience." ***Teilhard De Chardin***

As God's creatures, we are all connected on a spiritual level, and our physical presence on this earth is a temporary experience.

"Make every effort to keep the unity of the Spirit through the bond of peace." Ephesians 4:3

October 16

"When you feel like giving up remember that it's always too early to quit." ***Unknown***

Persisting until the end, and dealing with an undesirable outcome, is more noble than quitting due to the fear that you may fail.

"press on toward the goal to win the prize for which God has called me heavenward in Christ Jesus."
Philippians 3:14

October 17

"When you start seeing your worth, you'll stop seeing people who don't." ***Unknown***

When you are unable to realize your own value, you attract people into your life who undervalue you as well. You are a gem, an asset, a precious, irreplaceable soul. Once you have an understanding of who you really are, you will no longer build friendships with or do business with the wrong people.

"Indeed, the very hairs of your head are all numbered. Don't be afraid; you are worth more than many sparrows."
Luke 12:7

October 18

"A winner is a dreamer who never gives up."
Nelson Mandela

There's nothing in this life that can't be achieved if you are willing to do the work, stay the course, and be diligent enough follow through until the end.

"Blessed is the one who perseveres under trial because, having stood the test, that person will receive the crown of life that the Lord has promised to those who love him."
James 1:12

October 19

"The act of taking the first step is what separates the winners from the losers." ***Brian Tracy***

There's nothing like a great idea, but an idea means nothing unless you are willing to take the action required to implement it.

"May the favor of the Lord our God rest on us;
establish the work of our hands for us—
yes, establish the work of our hands." Psalms 90:17

October 20

"Only in the darkness can you see the stars."
Dr. Martin Luther King, Jr.

I often wonder what life would be like without heartache and trivia, and then I am quickly reminded that if we never experience hard times, we would have little or no gratitude for those times when everything in our lives are going well.

"Give thanks to the Lord, for he is good; his love endures forever." Psalms 107:1

October 21

"The best time to do something significant is between yesterday and tomorrow."
Zig Ziglar

When you get that burning desire to create something, or to take a particular action, don't waste too much time thinking about it. For me, those desires are often driven by a power greater than myself. Additionally, later on down the road, I realized that taking that action was the beginning of a major breakthrough for me.

"I will hasten and not delay to obey your commands."
Psalms 119:60

October 22

"Never let someone change who you are to become what they need." ***Unknown***

As God's creation, you are exactly who you were meant to be. God will continue to shape and mold you through life experiences. Do not pretend to be something or someone that another person wants you to be. If that person cannot accept you for who you are, they are probably not meant to be in your circle.

"For everything God created is good, and nothing is to be rejected if it is received with thanksgiving," 1 Timothy 4:4

October 23

"When life gives you lemons, make some lemon martinis!" ***Loni Mendez***

"You turned my wailing into dancing; you removed my sackcloth and clothed me with joy," Psalms 30:11

October 24

We need to do a better job at putting ourselves higher on our own to do list." ***Michelle Obama***

In order for us to care for others, we must take the best care of ourselves. If we don't eat well, get sufficient rest, and get enough movement, we will have nothing to offer to others.

"Don't you know that you yourselves are God's temple and that God's Spirit dwells in your midst?"
1 Corinthians 3:16

October 25

"If they don't give you a seat at the table, bring a folding chair." ***Shirley Chisholm***

Do not wait for co-workers, friends, or family members to commend you or validate your accomplishments. Continue to be led by your inner spirit, which provides you with God's guidance and direction.

"On the contrary, we speak as those approved by God to be entrusted with the gospel. We are not trying to please people but God, who tests our hearts."
1 Thessalonians 2:4

October 26

"If it's important to you you'll find a way, if it's not, you'll find an excuse." ***Ryan Blair***

Whenever someone tells me that I am too busy for them, my response is always the same: there is no such thing as too busy…people make time for whatever they want to make time for, and for the things that are meant to be.

Therefore do not be foolish, but understand what the Lord's will is." Ephesians 5:17

October 27

"All great achievements require time."
Maya Angelou

There is no such thing as an overnight success. When people emerge as great actors, great athletes, or great entertainers, what we haven't witnessed is all of the blood, sweat and tears that they've invested over an extended period of time.

"Be diligent in these matters; give yourself wholly to them, so that everyone may see your progress." 1 Timothy 4:15

October 28

"What you can do today can change all the tomorrows of your life." ***Zig Ziglar***

When you are looking to produce future results, the best thing you can do is take whatever action you can take today that will contribute to those results. Each day, do something that will move you closer to that desired outcome, and if your heart is really in it, you will manifest those results.

"For where your treasure is, there your heart will be also."
Matthew 6:21

October 29

"We are what we repeatedly do. Excellence then, is not an act but a habit." ***Aristotle***

Successful people have conditioned themselves by developing habits that raise the bar on their performance.

"who gave himself for us to redeem us from all wickedness and to purify for himself a people that are his very own, eager to do what is good." Titus 2:14

October 30

"Happiness is the real sense of fulfillment that comes from hard work." ***Joseph Barbara***

When you invest the time and effort, and put in the work that supports you in creating the life that you want, you experience a true sense of accomplishment and contentment.

"The fruit of the righteous is a tree of life, and the one who is wise saves lives." Proverbs 11:30

October 31

"Some people are driven by competition; I'm driven by purpose, fulfillment, and my standard when it comes to quality of life." ***Loni Mendez***

"Let us not become conceited, provoking and envying each other." Galatians 5:26

November 1

Happiness is not found, it's created. Choose to be joyful and happy today. The power to make that choice is a power that no one can take away from you." ***Loni Mendez***

"But the fruit of the Spirit is love, joy, peace, forbearance, kindness, goodness, faithfulness, Galatians 5:22

November 2

"A great man is hard on himself; a small man is hard on others." ***Confucius***

When you are in disagreement with someone, there is so much power in looking for ways that you could be responsible for the breakdown, rather than looking at the role that the other person played that contributed to the state of affairs.

"So watch yourselves. If your brother or sister sins against you, rebuke them; and if they repent, forgive them."
Luke 17:3

November 3

"We all make choices, but in the end our choices make us." ***Ken Levine***

The decisions that we make on a day-to-day basis and the knowledge that we acquire to support our goals, literally shape our futures.

"Desire without knowledge is not good—
how much more will hasty feet miss the way!"
Proverbs 19:2

November 4

"Life's most persistent and urgent question is, 'what are you doing for others?'"
Dr. Martin Luther King, Jr.

God gave each of us a purpose in life, and a major part of that purpose is to use our gifts, our talents, and our past experiences to contribute to others.

"And do not forget to do good and to share with others, for with such sacrifices God is pleased." Hebrews 13:16

November 5

"Shoot for the moon. Even if you miss, you'll land among the stars." ***Les Brown***

In setting goals, it is important that they are both measurable and achievable, but there is more value in setting stretch goals. These are the goals that will require major effort, and from which you will experience the most growth.

"He cuts off every branch in me that bears no fruit, while every branch that does bear fruit he prunes so that it will be even more fruitful." John 15:2

November 6

"He who knows all the answers has not been asked all the questions." ***Confucius***

No matter how many credentials you've been designated, or how much experience you have, there is always room for advice from the experts.

*"Plans fail for lack of counsel,
but with many advisers they succeed." Proverbs 15:22*

November 7

"A goal without a plan is only a dream."
Brian Tracy

Once you have determined what you want to do with your life, the next steps are to set your goals and create corresponding actions. Action is the most important part of the equation.

"Let perseverance finish its work so that you may be mature and complete, not lacking anything." James 1:4

November 8

"Dreams don't work unless you do."
John Maxwell

A dream is the start of a journey. What takes you from that starting point to the end result is the work that you do and the actions you take.

"Now finish the work, so that your eager willingness to do it may be matched by your completion of it, according to your means." 2 Corinthians 8:11

November 9

"It is impossible to keep it real when you are dealing with fake people!" ***Loni Mendez***

"He replied, "Isaiah was right when he prophesied about you hypocrites; as it is written: " 'These people honor me with their lips, but their hearts are far from me."
Mark 7:6

November 10

"I never dreamed about success, I worked for it." ***Estee Lauder***

Nothing can take the place of good, old fashioned hard work. It is the only way to accomplish your goals and dreams.

"The Lord God took the man and put him in the Garden of Eden to work it and take care of it." Genesis 2:15

November 11

"The road to success is always under construction." ***Steve Harvey***

When you are navigating your way toward reaching a major goal, it may seem like you are on a constant obstacle course. Consider that the path is designed that way for a reason, and that God has provided you with what you need to prevail.

"So do not fear, for I am with you; do not be dismayed, for I am your God. I will strengthen you and help you; I will uphold you with my righteous right hand."
Isaiah 41:10

November 12

"Where there is no vision, there is no hope."
George Washington Carver

In order for us to identify our specific steps to success, we must have a vision. It is impossible to reach an unidentified destination.

"Where there is no revelation, people cast off restraint; but blessed is the one who heeds wisdom's instruction."
Proverbs 29:18

November 13

"There is no greater agony than bearing an untold story inside of you." ***Maya Angelou***

Communication is everything, and when we hold things inside it stops us from moving forward in many places in our lives.

"The righteous cry out, and the Lord hears them; he delivers them from all their troubles." Psalms 34:17

November 14

"Live out your imagination, not your history."
Stephen Covey

There is so much to look forward to in life. If we use our energy to create a future for ourselves, we will have less energy to focus on things of the past.

"Let your eyes look straight ahead; fix your gaze directly before you." Proverbs 4:25

November 15

"I'm sure that we can all write a long list of things that aren't going the way we want them to or that we aren't happy with, and we could do this with little to no effort. But think about the power in writing a list of things that we have to be grateful for, starting with the fact that today is another day that we are living and breathing, and that we are all equipped to make things happen. We just need to believe that we can." ***Loni Mendez***

"Give thanks to the Lord, for he is good; his love endures forever." 1 Chronicles 16:34

November 16

"Either I'll find a way, or I will make one."
Philip Sidney

When you are determined to accomplish something, you find a way to make it happen.

"This is what the Lord says— he who made a way through the sea, a path through the mighty waters,"
Isaiah 43:16

November 17

"Not everything that is faced can be changed, but nothing can be changed until it is faced."
James Baldwin

The start of improving a situation is being honest with ourselves and acknowledging that improvement is necessary.

"The wisdom of the prudent is to give thought to their ways, but the folly of fools is deception." Proverbs 14:8

November 18

"We can never obtain peace in the outer world until we make peace with ourselves."
Dalai Lama

When you are not content with your own life, seeking peace outside of yourself is a moot point. What there is to do is take a long, hard look at your life to determine the source of the discontent.

"Let us therefore make every effort to do what leads to peace and to mutual edification." Romans 14:19

November 19

"Abundance is a process of letting go; that which is empty can receive." ***Bryant H. McGill***

Whether it is food, money, or material possessions that you are storing, hoarding is a matter of the mind. If we hold on to things for fear that we won't have enough, it has the opposite effect on our lives. The key to having more is to let go of the fear that you will be without.

"For we brought nothing into the world, and we can take nothing out of it." 1 Timothy 6:7

November 20

"Never lose the opportunity to see something beautiful, for beauty is God's handwriting."
Ralph Waldo Emerson

Every now and then, stop what you're doing and bring your hectic life to a halt for about five minutes. Take in all of the beautiful things that are surrounding you…the sun, the greenery, the blue sky…it's a powerful practice that helps you to stay grounded.

"From Zion, perfect in beauty, God shines forth."
Psalms 50:2

November 21

"Winners are losers who got up and gave it one more try." ***Dennis Deyoung***

When you think about giving up, just imagine how frustrating it would be if you found out later that you were just about there when you gave up.

"Do you not know that in a race all the runners run, but only one gets the prize? Run in such a way as to get the prize." 1 Corinthians 9:24

November 22

"A dream becomes a goal when action is taken toward its achievement." ***Bo Bennett***

The way to fulfill on the things you want for yourself is to write that dream down, write down the corresponding goal, write down the actions that you need to take to achieve that goal, and take one of those actions every day.

"Then the Lord replied: "Write down the revelation and make it plain on tablets so that a herald may run with it." Habakkuk 2:2

November 23

"Gratitude, like faith, is a muscle. The more you use it, the stronger it grows."
Alan Cohen

When you practice gratitude, you are letting the universe know that you want more of what you are thankful for.

"Give thanks to the Lord, for he is good; his love endures forever." 1 Chronicles 15:34

November 24

"It always seems impossible until it's done."
Nelson Mandela

Everything occurred as impossible at one point in the past. This is evident when we look at all of the technology that we are able to take advantage of today. At one point, those things seemed ureal and unattainable. They are a reality today because someone had the wherewithal to take action, and operate from a place of possibility.

"Jesus replied, "What is impossible with man is possible with God." Luke 18:27

November 25

"You must never be fearful about what you are doing when it is right." ***Rosa Parks***

When you get to a place where you doubt whether you are doing the right thing, rely on your inner spirit to guide you.

'Whether you turn to the right or to the left, your ears will hear a voice behind you, saying, "This is the way; walk in it." Isaiah 30:21

November 26

"People with goals succeed because they know where they're going." ***Earl Nightingale***

A roadmap is a must when you venture out on the road to that next level in your life. When you couple that roadmap with prayer and patience, it is impossible to fail.

"Be joyful in hope, patient in affliction, faithful in prayer." Romans 12:12

November 27

"When you turn your passions into profit and design your life so that you are doing what you love every day, you will never have to 'work' again!"

Loni Mendez

"We have different gifts, according to the grace given to each of us. If your gift is prophesying, then prophesy in accordance with your faith;" Romans 12:6

November 28

"God will not take you someplace that won't sustain you." ***Joel Osteen***

When you feel like giving up, remember that you are not alone, and that there is an underlying purpose to what you are going through.

"I consider that our present sufferings are not worth comparing with the glory that will be revealed in us." Romans 8:18

November 29

"Good leaders know their strengths, but great leaders know the strengths of their people."
Unknown

Those whom God has given the gift of leadership are summoned to touch and inspire others, and to have an impact on their lives.

"Let everyone be subject to the governing authorities, for there is no authority except that which God has established. The authorities that exist have been established by God." Romans 13:1

November 30

"Until you value yourself, you will not value your time; Until you value your time, you will not value anyone else's time!"
Loni Mendez

"Be very careful, then, how you live—not as unwise but as wise, making the most of every opportunity, because the days are evil." Ephesians 5:15-16

December 1

"Confidence is silent, insecurities are loud."
Unknown

When you feel like you are lacking confidence, draw on your past successes. They provide the proof that you can prevail.

"So do not throw away your confidence; it will be richly rewarded." Hebrews 10:35

December 2

"There's nothing wrong with ordinary, I just prefer to shoot for extraordinary." ***Darren Hardy***

God created us to be extraordinary human beings. This is the gift that He gave us along with the gift of life.

"I praise you because I am fearfully and wonderfully made; your works are wonderful, I know that full well."
Psalms 139:14

December 3

"Never allow yourself to play small to fit into someone else's life. If the game you're playing in life is too big for them, consider that they're not the one!" ***Loni Mendez***

"Therefore, my brothers and sisters, make every effort to confirm your calling and election. For if you do these things, you will never stumble," 2 Peter 1:10

December 4

"One way to let go of the past is to realize that it served you and that it was a necessary part of the journey to where you are today."
Aaron Daugherty

God nudges us in the direction in which He wants us to go. Sometimes, we must go through certain things in order to get where we need to get. Once we've gotten through those things, we must look straight ahead and continue on the path that is meant for us, thus leaving the past behind.

"he refreshes my soul. He guides me along the right paths for his name's sake." Psalms 23:3

December 5

"Change is the parent of progress."
Steve Maraboli

Nothing in life stays the same. If we resist change, we resist the evolution of who we are, and who we are meant to become.

"Create in me a pure heart, O God, and renew a steadfast spirit within me." Psalms 51:10

December 6

"It is support that sustains us on the journey we've started." ***Marci Shimoff***

It's nice to have the support of family and friends for the decisions that we make in life. But there will be times when those closest to us are not in agreement with our choices. During those times the gift of discernment will reveal to us whether it is the direction in which God wants us to go. And if so, His support is all that we need.

"Surely God is my help; the Lord is the one who sustains me." Psalms 54:4

December 7

"Sometimes you just really have to stop holding on for dear life and let God do His work!! "
Loni Mendez

"The Lord will fight for you; you need only to be still."
Exodus 14:14

December 8

"The future is nothing more than a continuation of present moments."
Ralph Smart

When you develop the ability to be present each moment of the day, learning to remain focused will compliment that ability, and you will be proud of the future that you are creating, moment by moment.

"Since no one knows the future, who can tell someone else what is to come?" Ecclesiastes 8:7

December 9

"Possibility has a short shelf life and must, therefore, be generated on an ongoing basis."
Loni Mendez

"I am the Lord, the God of all mankind. Is anything too hard for me?" Jeremiah 32:27

December 10

"Your greatest resource is your time."
Brian Tracy

When you wake up every morning, plan how you are going to use your time. Once it's gone you cannot get it back.

"As long as it is day, we must do the works of him who sent me. Night is coming, when no one can work."
John 9:4

December 11

"Punctuality is the soul of business."
Thomas Chandler Haliburton

If you want to be successful in life, be early for everything. Live by the motto that "on time" is late.

"There is a time for everything, and a season for every activity under the heavens:" Ecclesiastes 3:1

December 12

"In the process of letting go you will lose many things from the past, but you will find yourself."
Deepak Chopra

A valuable life lesson teaches us that we can't hoard material possessions. When we are willing to purge by donating items that we no longer need, we open doors and make space for new beginnings.

"All day long he craves for more, but the righteous give without sparing." Proverbs 21:26

December 13

"Through the eyes of gratitude everything is a miracle." ***Mary Davis***

Gratitude cultivates abundance. When we are thankful for all that we have, it sends the message that we are able to receive more miracles from Him.

"Sing to the Lord with grateful praise; make music to our God on the harp." Psalms 147:7

December 14

"Good things happen when you set your priorities straight." ***Scott Caan***

Take a look at your calendar for an entire month, in order to evaluate how you spend your time every day. Because time is such a precious treasure, this is a great way to assess whether you are spending your time on the things that are most important to you.

"For where your treasure is, there your heart will be also."
Luke 12:34

December 15

"Everything that happens to you is for your growth." ***Robin Sharma***

Consider that often when things happen to us, they provide us with an experience that equips us to minister to someone else down the road, who is going through the same situation.

"It is my pleasure to tell you about the miraculous signs and wonders that the Most High God has performed for me." Daniel 4:2

December 16

"If you don't let your past die, your past won't let you live." ***Unknown***

Holding on to events of the past does not serve you. By doing so, you are interfering with your own growth and development, and the plans for your future.

"Get rid of all bitterness, rage and anger, brawling and slander, along with every form of malice." *Ephesians 4:31*

December 17

"The greatest threat to our planet is the belief that someone else will save it." ***Robert Swan***

We each have a responsibility to participate in sustaining our habitat. If we don't care for our land today, it will no longer exist for the generations to come.

"I brought you into a fertile land to eat its fruit and rich produce. But you came and defiled my land and made my inheritance detestable." Jeremiah 2:7

December 18

"Beauty begins the moment you decide to be yourself." ***Coco Chanel***

Your beauty has two components: your spirit and soul, which are on the inside, and the way you carry yourself, which is visible on the outside.

"Your beauty should not come from outward adornment, such as elaborate hairstyles and the wearing of gold jewelry or fine clothes. 4 Rather, it should be that of your inner self, the unfading beauty of a gentle and quiet spirit, which is of great worth in God's sight." 1 Peter 3:3-4

December 19

"If you can do what you do best and be happy, you are further along in life than most people."
Leonardo DiCaprio

While there are many things that we simply must endure in life, the painful events do not define life in its entirety. Let us not lose sight that it is a journey that is meant for us to cherish and enjoy.

"All who are skilled among you are to come and make everything the Lord has commanded" Exodus 35:10

December 20

"Activity leads to productivity."
Jim Rohn

When working towards an accomplishment, the main ingredient is action. Even if you take action and you discover that it is the wrong action, at least you have identified what doesn't work. You can then move on to the next action, and keep trying until you get it right.

"Be sure you know the condition of your flocks, give careful attention to your herds;" Proverbs 27:23

December 21

"Don't be upset when it seems as if someone disappeared from your life. Sometimes God takes the trash out for you." ***Unknown***

Be cautious of keeping company with people with negative energy; people who participate in excessive gossip or who live unproductive lives. It's not that the actual person is unfit for your company, but its their behavior that you can do without, and that needs to be disposed of.

"Do not be misled: "Bad company corrupts good character." 1 Corinthians 15:33

December 22

"You may think there is a lot wrong with you, but there is also a lot right with you."
Joel Osteen

Accepting who you are is a critical component of living your best life. No one is perfect, as we all have our flaws. However, we also have gifts, talents and the ability to be the contribution to the world that God meant for us to be.

"But you are a chosen people, a royal priesthood, a holy nation, God's special possession, that you may declare the praises of him who called you out of darkness into his wonderful light." 1 Peter 2:9

December 23

"The starting point of all achievement is desire."
Napoleon Hill

When you have a burning desire in your heart, it has moved past the point of origin, which is a mere thought. At that point, what there is to do is to make a plan and take the action that is necessary to make it happen.

"May He give you the desires of your heart and make all your plans succeed." Psalms 20:4

December 24

"The beautiful thing about learning is that no one can take it away from you." ***BB King***

Learning is a critical part of existing. If you are not learning on an ongoing basis, you are simply not being the best you that you can be.

"And Jesus grew in wisdom and stature, and in favor with God and man." Luke 2:52

December 25

"We must travel in the direction of our fear."
John Berryman

When we are committed to facing our fears, it indicates that we are willing to develop ourselves.

"There is no fear in love. But perfect love drives out fear, because fear has to do with punishment. The one who fears is not made perfect in love." 1 John 4:18

December 26

"It's the little details that are vital. Little things make big things happen." ***John Wooden***

When you are facing a monumental task, try not to look at the entire task at once. Instead, try dividing it into smaller tasks, and focusing on those one at a time.

"Let your eyes look straight ahead; fix your gaze directly before you." Proverbs 4:25

December 27

"Don't judge each day by the harvest you reap,
but by the seeds that you plant."
Robert Louis Stevenson

There are times when we may not see the results of the actions we take until much later. These are considered actions that plant seeds that we will benefit from down the road.

"Peacemakers who sow in peace reap a harvest of righteousness." James 3:18

December 28

"The wisest mind has something yet to learn."
George Santayana

As long as we are living, no matter how much reading we do, how much exploring we do, or how many degrees we achieve, there will always be more to learn. To live is to grow.

"Instruct the wise and they will be wiser still;
teach the righteous and they will add to their learning."
Proverbs 9:9

December 29

"If you're searching for that one person that will change your life, take a look in the mirror."
Unknown

When it comes to making changes in our lives, we are the only ones who have the power to do that. Not only do we ourselves have to want the change, but we are also the only ones who can do the work to make it happen.

"for each one should carry their own load." Galatians 6:5

December 30

"What looks like a crystal-clear path to you may look like a murky mess to others...stay focused, you have what it takes to get through. They won't see it because God gave you the task...not them."
Loni Mendez

"Before I formed you in the womb I knew you, before you were born I set you apart; I appointed you as a prophet to the nations." Jeremiah 1:5

December 31

"The groundwork of all happiness is good health." ***James Leigh Hunt***

Without our health there isn't much that we can accomplish. Therefore, it is an absolute priority that we take the best care of ourselves.

"Dear friend, I pray that you may enjoy good health and that all may go well with you, even as your soul is getting along well." 3 John 1:2

Made in United States
Orlando, FL
29 January 2022

14205114R00205